The delightful book that answers the questions...

- Why is my home being invaded by bats? And how can I make them find somewhere else to live?

- Why is the great horned owl one of the few predators to regularly dine on skunk?

- What are the three reasons you may have weasels around your house but never see them?

- What event in the middle of winter will bring possums out in full force?

- What common Michigan animal has been dubbed "the most feared mammal on the North American continent"?

- Why would we be wise to shun the cute little mouse and welcome a big black snake?

- Why should you be very careful where you stack the firewood?

MSU is an Affirmative-Action Equal Opportunity Institution. Cooperative Extension Service programs are open to all without regard to race, color, national origin, sex or handicap.
Issued in furtherance of Cooperative Extension work in agriculture and home economics, acts of May 8, and June 30, 1914, in cooperation with the U.S. Department of Agriculture, Gail L. Imig, director, Cooperative Extension Service, Michigan State University, E. Lansing, MI 48824.

Produced by Outreach Communications

MICHIGAN STATE
U N I V E R S I T Y

Extension Bulletin E-2323
ISBN 1-56525-000-1

NATURE
from
YOUR BACK DOOR

By

Glenn R. Dudderar

Extension Wildlife Specialist
Michigan State University

with

Leslie Johnson

Outreach Communications
Michigan State University

Illustrations by

Brenda Shear

FIRST EDITION — AUTUMN 1991

INTRODUCTION

When I came to Michigan in the mid-1970s, I was surprised at the prevailing attitude that nature and wildlife were things to see and enjoy if you went "up north". Admittedly, that was my first impression when I saw from the air the greater Detroit metropolitan sprawl and the scattered woodlots of mid-Michigan farm country.

I soon learned otherwise. Of course, cedar swamps, bear, elk, moose, fishers and sprawling forests occur only in the north country, but southern Michigan has bogs, deer, bobcats and even a few beaver and bald eagles, as well as oak-hickory woods and a great variety and abundance of less glamorous wildlife. Even the common cottontail rabbit, raccoon, robin and, yes, even the house sparrow, have fascinating and little known features that can delight and even amaze the astute observer.

When I made a comment along these lines to Bob Neumann, the agricultural writer at what was then MSU's Information Services, he suggested we write a monthly column about backyard nature and wildlife. The column was an instant success and is now published in about 200 newsletters, newspapers and magazines around the state and occasionally adapted for publication out of state. When Bob's job duties changed, Leslie Johnson became my editor, and over the past 13 years, we have produced more than 140 monthly columns. In 1990, Leslie suggested that we edit selected columns and combine them into a book that would further our goal of helping Michigan residents better understand, appreciate and enjoy the wildlife that shares their daily lives. Thus this book came into being.

Compiling the book was easy compared with writing the monthly columns. The usual problem of any column is what to write about that's new, different, timely, interesting and illuminating. Frequently, a telephone call provides a topic.

As an Extension specialist for the MSU Department of Fisheries and Wildlife, I receive many telephone inquiries about wildlife. These often evolve into columns. For example, when someone called to ask about a 10-inch brown and yellow animal that looked like a small dinosaur, I knew the next column would be "The March Tiger", a story about Michigan's tiger salamander.

(Unfortunately, that column was written before we started saving them, so it doesn't appear in this book.)

Timeliness is often difficult, especially when the Upper Peninsula is still buried in snow and ice and southern Michigan is experiencing a balmy early spring. And when unusual weather causes unusual and fascinating wildlife phenomena, the column is, of course, up to a month late reporting on it. Relevance is another problem. Beaver in your backyard is certainly relevant to residents of the U.P. and northern Michigan, but not to folks in southern Michigan — not yet, at least. Making the column applicable to the whole state is difficult even for universal topics such as backyard bird feeding. Some birds that visit bird feeders (e.g., pine grosbeaks) come south to the U.P. for most winters, while southern Michigan is too far north in the winter for other birds (e.g., chipping sparrows).

Combining accuracy and readability is another concern. When working on a column about how birds recognize their young or food, I might say, "As an order, birds have less acute olfactory abilities than mammals and they therefore rely primarily on visual recognition." True enough, but to make that jargon-laden professional statement more readable, Leslie would write, "Birds generally do not have a very sharp sense of smell, so they recognize their young (or food) by sight." We often struggle to maintain that easy readability without producing an oversimplified column that prompts huffy letters from learned ornithologists informing us that some birds can detect certain odors very well and may even use their sense of smell to help them navigate during migration. Frequently, Leslie thinks we need more detail rather than less. When I wrote that Michigan's gray tree frogs are almost as good as chameleons in changing color but that very few people know about them while every school child knows about chameleons, she asked where chameleons come from. That seemingly simple question led to several productive hours of research on lizards, anoles and chameleons and the task of resolving all that information into a non-technical sentence or two.

Accuracy also changes with time. Some of the columns in this book were written over 10 years ago, and recent research required that some be revised and updated. Although that made putting this book together more difficult, it is reassuring to know that research will continue to produce new information that can become topics for future columns.

— Glenn Dudderar   *July 1991*

P.S.: Brenda Shear, who made the delightful illustrations for this book, has asked us to thank Mike Jackson for allowing her to draw the opossum on page 61 from his award-winning photo and Harper Collins for the same use of photos from the books "World of the White Tailed Deer" and "World of the Racoon."

Chapter I
Scenes of Michigan Seasons

APRIL - A TRANSITION TIME

APRIL AND EARLY MAY ARE A TIME OF TRANSITION IN Michigan. The brown of the winter landscape gives way to green, and the spring migration is in full swing.

One of the outstanding sights of April is the passage of the tundra swans across Michigan. They follow a path that runs across the state from Detroit to Muskegon. In late March and early April, they migrate from their wintering grounds around Chesapeake Bay to nesting sites in Canada's Northwest Territory.

They may show up in farmers' fields, along streams or in marshes. They look much like the large white swans we often see in parks. Those are mute swans, which are domestic swans from Europe. The whistling swan is native to this continent. Rural residents often see them resting or feeding in large fields. City residents may hear their high-pitched call and look up to see a bright white V against the blue sky of a sunny early April day.

Another bird that you may see passing through is the ruddy turnstone. This bird, in its bright rusty red, black and white courtship plumage, is on its way from the Gulf of Mexico, where it spent the winter, to its nesting territory inside the Arctic Circle. Lakeshore residents often see the bird on jetties, rocks and stony beaches, searching for food under small stones that it overturns with its beak.

The birds that spend their summers in Michigan begin to trickle in during March, but many more, such as the purple martin and wren, arrive in April. For the backyard naturalist, this means it's time to put out or clean up the birdhouses. When the leading edge of the migration arrives, the males will start scouting for likely nest sites.

The birds that return to Michigan in April usually have it easier than the early birds that arrive in early March. When the earliest returnees arrive, food supplies are pretty much depleted. The robins and other birds flocking in during April, however, can take advantage of the hordes of earthworms forced out of the ground by warm April rains.

Songbirds aren't the only creatures on hand to take advantage of this food bonanza. The ducks on the MSU campus can often be seen

waddling along sidewalks and roads, gulping worms as fast as they can snap them up.

A lot of birds conduct their courtships in April before settling down on the nest to incubate eggs and rear young ones. If you're lucky enough to live near a wetland area inhabited by sandhill cranes, you may get to observe their courtship dance. It begins with a stately minuet that gradually builds to a disco crescendo. The woodcock does his wooing in the sky, looping and diving to impress his prospective lady. Once on the ground, usually in a field near aspen trees, he struts, bobs and dips, periodically giving a short buzzy call.

Birds aren't the only creatures to return to our yards and fields after a sojourn elsewhere. Ground squirrels and bats, which hibernated all winter, and moles, which were tunneling deep in the soil, will be

making their presence known again in April.

Worms, beetles, grubs and other small animals in the soil are the main items on the mole's menu. When the soil begins to warm up and these creatures become active, I know the telephone calls about moles burrowing in lawns and gardens are not far behind.

April is often the month when people find out they have been living with bats all winter. When bats first break hibernation, they're quite likely to blunder into home living areas.

Ground squirrels come out of winter quarters about the same time that the spring bulbs send up shoots. For the squirrels, the flowers are a convenient source of food. Gardeners, who are also pretty hungry for flowers by this time, though in a different way, aren't likely to welcome the foragers.

Skunks, opossums and raccoons are even pushier than ground squirrels. They're looking for dens where they can raise their young, and in urban and suburban areas where hollow trees are in short supply, they often move right in with humans. Ordinarily the homeowner doesn't know he has boarders until the young animals get big enough to romp around, usually in May. But the actual invasion occurs in late March or early April.

In northern Michigan, the bears bring their young out of the dens around April, and the beavers begin building and rebuilding their dams. Both animals sometimes make nuisances out of themselves in the spring, the bears by raiding beehives, and the beavers by damming streams so that they back up and flood roads and fields.

Fortunately, the frogs that come out of hibernation in early spring are destructive only to the quiet of an April evening. To someone who doesn't care for their singing, of course, the racket created by the frogs in every puddle and ditch can be a disturbance. Swimming pool owners may find their pools invaded by hordes of frogs and toads and the filters clogged by masses of gelatinous eggs. Toads can be foiled by a six-inch barrier around the pool. A little higher barrier will keep out some frogs, but tree frogs, with their suction cup toes, can climb almost any surface. Starting to filter and chlorinate the water early in the spring may be necessary to control them.

Frogs in swimming pools, bats in bedrooms and moles in lawns make April frog, bat and mole month for me, but I also get a lot of calls about abandoned or orphaned baby animals. Most of these animal babies are neither orphaned nor abandoned — most times, the parents are close by, waiting for the meddling humans to go away so they can get back to tending their young. But people get concerned when they find babies alone.

They're likely to find these animals because people, too, are breaking a sort of winter dormant period, taking advantage of the weather to work outside in the lawn or garden or hike in the woods and fields. This naturally increases their chances of coming into contact with some kind of wild animal.

We're also seeing wild animals moving into the suburban areas developed in the '50s and '60s. As the landscape plantings in these areas mature, they become more attractive to small animals and birds. With wild animals as near neighbors, people can observe quite a slice of nature from their back doors.

SNAKES UNDERFOOT

DURING THE TIME BETWEEN MID-APRIL AND MID-MAY, MANY PEOPLE witness a dramatic — and to some, traumatic — phenomenon in their backyards: large numbers of snakes coming out of hibernation.

Warm days bring snakes out of the places where they've spent the winter hibernating. Because snakes can not regulate their body temperature internally, they are sluggish and slow moving during cool weather. Later in the summer, they'll quickly slither away from us, often unnoticed, but in the early spring, they move away slowly, if at all. People used to having wild animals scurry out of their way may become alarmed because the snakes don't seem to be afraid and don't move off.

It doesn't help if there seem to be large numbers of snakes underfoot, as if the backyard had been invaded by snakes.

What's actually happening, of course, is that the snakes that entered the hibernaculum (the hibernation place) one at a time, unobserved, tend to come out of it all at once. One day there are no snakes in the yard — the next, there seem to be snakes everywhere. It's logical for the homeowner to surmise that the snakes came into the backyard from somewhere outside it.

The truth is that they probably hibernated there — underground in a cavity next to a stone foundation or stone retaining wall — and are on their way out.

Depending on the weather and available food, the snakes may scatter quickly or hang around for a few days or a week. Cool weather may chase them back into their sheltered spot, to emerge again when temperatures rise. A good supply of their favorite foods — earthworms in the case of garter snakes; rodents for milk snakes — may encourage them to stay in the yard for a while.

If this backyard snake population includes large numbers of small (6 to 8 inches) snakes, the homeowner may get the impression that snakes are living and breeding in the house. This is not something to worry about. Young snakes are hatched or born in the late summer. Any small snakes you see in the spring are last summer's babies.

Unfortunately, most people are afraid of snakes, even the harmless garter snakes that are the most likely species to inhabit or pass through a backyard. Understanding that most snakes are harmless and even helpful, in that they eat worms, insects and rodents, enables some people to tolerate having them around. But even someone who appreciates snakes' place in the natural scheme of things may be startled when he encounters a snake close to home.

When it's 40 to 60 snakes, even the most snake-tolerant person can get a little uneasy. Then if a snake or two blunders into the house instead of out into the yard, my phone is likely to ring and someone will be asking, "What can I do to get rid of these snakes?"

There are no quick and easy solutions to what some people see as their backyard snake problem. If you can tolerate the presence of the snakes for a few days, they'll leave on their own.

Snakes in the house are another matter, of course. My preference would be to trap and release them outdoors. You can make a snake trap by fastening plastic glue trays, sold to trap rodents, on boards and placing the boards wherever snakes are likely to crawl. When a snake is caught by the glue trap, take it outside and pour vegetable oil on the trap. The oil will release the glue's hold on the snake. If you feel you must kill the snake, kill it while it is trapped.

Fumigation by a pest control operator will kill snakes in the house, but it is extremely expensive. And it leaves your house with dead snakes and other creatures. This approach is hardly worthwhile unless it is the only thing that will give you peace of mind.

If one snake happened to get inside, there's probably nothing to stop other snakes, as well as rodents, insects and other creatures, from

coming in by the same opening. So the long-term solution to a lot of pest problems is to inspect the foundation, fill in any cavities where snakes might hibernate, and seal up any cracks or gaps through which they might find their way inside.

Perhaps one of the most interesting things about snakes is the various ways people react to them and to my explanation of what the snakes are doing in their yards.

Someone who sees all snakes as a threat and fears even photos of snakes in magazines won't be very happy with my advice to relax and let the snakes clear out of the yard on their own.

Other people seem to enjoy being afraid of snakes and are disappointed when they understand there are no snake invasions, no snakes breeding and living in the house, and no reason to be afraid.

Still others are simply fascinated with this opportunity to observe snakes close up. They realize that Michigan snakes are not any more dangerous than the birds that come to a backyard feeder, the one exception being the massasauga rattlesnake, which lives in swamps and marshes and rarely uses the backyard habitat. With this understanding, they can tolerate and even enjoy these scaly residents of the backyard nature preserve.

STORMY WEATHER

WHEN MICHIGAN'S WEATHER GETS VIOLENT, WE HUMANS HEAD for shelter. When we come out, we often find that the storm has dropped some furred or feathered visitors into our backyards.

By midsummer, there are all sorts of young animals and birds at various stages of development in trees, on roofs, and in and around buildings. We may not know they're around until a storm reveals them to us.

For instance, one midsummer storm some years ago in late July toppled hundreds of trees, including a big old oak tree in Williamston. In a hollow of that tree was a nest of young sparrow hawks. No one had any idea sparrow hawks had nested in that tree. But there they were.

In this case, the young birds were able to fly and abandoned the destroyed nest cavity with their parents. The young nighthawk that blew off the flat roof of a building on the MSU campus in the same storm was not so well developed. It still needed to be protected and fed by the parent birds. Its mother tried to care for it on the ground, but passers-by frightened her away before she could be netted and placed back on the roof with her young one. Rescuers eventually carried the youngster to the roof and placed it where they hoped the mother bird would find it.

That storm also blew the roof off a shed in rural Ingham County, revealing five baby raccoons between the inside and outside walls. Judging from their size — about 6 inches long — they must have been born in June.

The owner of the shed called me to find out what she should do about the young raccoons. There was no reason to believe the mother had died or deserted her young, so I suggested that the woman wait and watch to see what happened. Sure enough, the mother raccoon was soon scuttling from the old den to some new hiding place. She made five trips, one for each kit.

Before I came to Michigan, I was on hand when a nest of nine baby barn owls was removed from a silo destroyed by a storm. The birds were at the ball of fluff stage and could not survive on their own, so volunteers were found to try to raise them. Those that survived to adulthood were trained to fly and hunt and then released.

Barn owls are an endangered species in Michigan, so it would be unusual to find a nest of them victimized by a storm, but it's not unusual for a big wind to blow baby squirrels, doves or robins out of a tree.

Doves and robins may nest and raise young two or three times in the spring and summer. Squirrels may have a nest of young anytime from March to October. So anytime there are trees coming down in a summer storm, you may have baby birds and squirrels coming down with them.

Residents of suburban neighborhoods are often surprised to find flying squirrels in fallen trees. Because these animals are active at night, most people never see them, even though most neighborhoods with large trees have them. The squirrels are discovered when a nest is spilled out on the ground or opened when a fallen tree is sawed up.

Doves' nests get strewn about every time a strong summer wind comes up because of the way they're built. The dove makes a loose platform of sticks to lay its eggs on. When the wind blows hard, sticks and eggs or baby birds often go flying. The parents then make another pile of sticks and start over. With both doves and robins, this starting over can go on through the summer, long after the time we usually think of as the nesting and baby bird season.

Though high winds are usually the main problem for wildlife caught in a storm, heavy rains can also take their toll. It's not uncommon for young quail, pheasants and other ground birds, soaked by a downpour, to get chilled and die. When the rain comes down so hard that it runs along the ground in a sheet, baby rabbits may drown in their nests.

Young birds and animals aren't the only ones to suffer in bad weather. Occasionally adult birds get blown off their perches by a high wind, caught by a storm as they fly or forced down to the ground by bad weather. Birds trapped in the eye of a hurricane, for instance, have to go with the storm until it dissipates. In Michigan, water birds like the cormorant may get caught by a storm and driven down into the middle of the state, far from their usual haunts. The sudden presence of this odd-looking bird generally produces unusual responses from inland residents.

Probably the most unusual thing to find after a storm is a

backyard full of fish. This can happen when a waterspout sucks up fish from a lake or pond and transports them across country. When the water spout dissipates, the fish rain out of the sky, sometimes far from water. Most people are incredulous.

Even if you never see a waterspout or a rain of fish, you're likely to see plenty of violent storms and their effects on Michigan wildlife. It's all part of the changing panorama of nature from your back door.

BEATING THE HEAT

IF YOU THINK YOU GET HOT DURING THE SUMMER WHEN temperatures top 90 degrees, think what it must be like for creatures with permanent fur coats or down jackets — and no fans or air conditioners!

Animals and birds have devised several ways of coping with the heat. Some are physiological; some are behavioral.

One strategy for coping with the heat that you can readily see in your backyard occurs in birds. They sit with their bills open and their wings spread away from their bodies to try to get rid of excess heat. Uncovering the featherless skin under each wing helps increase air circulation over the skin. Though they don't exactly pant as a dog does, they also get rid of excess body heat as they exhale through their open mouths.

Another thing birds do is lose their feathers. I get calls every summer from people asking about bald-headed birds. All species lose feathers (molt), but most of us don't look closely enough at birds often enough to recognize that some do not immediately replace all molted feathers. If the skin underneath is the same color as the feathers, we may not notice that feathers are missing and bare skin is exposed. When the skin is a different color, the loss of feathers is very obvious.

One question I get every year around mid-August is "Where have all the male mallards gone?" The truth is that they're around

■

— they've just lost their striking green, white and maroon feathers and replaced them with drab, ratty-looking feathers that make them look more like the less colorful female ducks. Those feathers, in turn, give way to the colorful plumage that we think of as the typical male mallard colors. All this feather shedding and regrowing occurs in July and August, so for two months, male mallards don't look quite put together.

Mammals do similar things. Anyone who has a dog with a fluffy undercoat knows what mammals do in summer: they lose their insulating underfur.

Also like dogs, many mammals — including squirrels and raccoons — pant in hot weather to eliminate body heat.

One mammal you're likely to see frequently in your backyard is the rabbit. Look closely at the next one you see on a hot day. Its ears will probably look wider and pinker than usual, and it will be holding them up and away from its body. The ears are engorged with blood — that accounts for their pink color. They act as radiators for the animal, allowing body heat to dissipate into the air. In the winter, the rabbit partially folds its ears lengthwise and carries them close to its body to conserve heat.

An obvious behavioral approach to cooling is birds' taking baths. Though they may have many reasons for bathing, we have to speculate that one of them in summer is to cool down. Matting their feathers with water exposes more skin and so improves air circulation. Evaporative cooling also occurs as the feathers dry.

A most common mammalian behavior is not doing anything. Rabbits sprawl under a bush in the shade; squirrels drape themselves over tree branches and swing in the breeze. Rabbits will also dig a shallow hole in the shade and lie in the cool earth. The woodchuck will spend the hottest parts of the day in its cool burrow, coming out only early and late in the day.

The aim, of course, is to minimize movement and heat generation and absorption. The absence of animals that you ordinarily see is your tipoff that they're holed up somewhere trying to keep cool.

Birds and mammals also consume more water in the summer. A birdbath in your yard may attract a tremendous amount of attention from not only birds that ordinarily wouldn't visit a feeder but an assortment of mammals: chipmunks, squirrels, ground squirrels, rabbits and about any other animal frequently seen in the backyard. Though ground squirrels can get all the water they need from their feed, they will take advantage of a source of fresh water for cooling.

Humans who don't rely on air conditioning to keep cool use many of these same behaviors to beat the heat. We wear fewer, lighter clothes; go swimming; sit in the shade with a cool lemonade; avoid strenuous work in the heat of the day; and take cool showers. When heat and humidity are stifling, it's easy to empathize with the furred and feathered creatures you can see as you observe nature from your back door.

SEPTEMBER — A SECOND SPRING

MOST PEOPLE THINK OF SEPTEMBER AS A WINDING-DOWN TIME. It's the end of the summer and the end of the growing season — crops are being harvested, leaves will soon turn color and fall, and birds will be migrating. It's a time for ending and wrapping up and getting ready for winter.

We don't often think of September as a time of beginning, of new life. But in some ways, that's exactly what it is.

You can see right in your backyard some of the changes that occur in September. Like spring, it's a fantastic time to enjoy the changes going on. And you will see many springlike scenes.

If you feed birds, you will notice baby goldfinches being fed by their parents. The young on the ground will beg from the adults, which fly to the feeder, get sunflower or thistle seeds, and take them back to the young and feed them. It may appear that goldfinches are raising their young out of season, but if you bear in mind that their primary food is thistle seed and that thistle seed matures in the late summer and early fall, their timing suddenly seems quite sensible. They are raising their young at the time when their favorite food is most readily available.

September is also the month when you're likely to see young gray and fox squirrels coming out of the nest for the first time. These are often the second litters of the year. If nuts are abundant, these young squirrels may be better off than those born in the spring, when food was harder to come by. In a good nut year, these youngsters can put on a lot of fat and stash a supply of food to get them through their first winter.

We usually think of spring as the prime time for wildflowers, and that's true of the woodland wildflowers. But a tremendous blooming of meadow wildflowers occurs in September. Sometimes we get so caught up in the spectacle of the fall foliage colors that we overlook the wildflowers. One group I find particularly beautiful is the asters. Each plant looks like a bouquet waiting to be popped into a vase. The large, showy flowers decorate fields and roadsides in the fall with shades of red, blue, purple, lavender and white. The golden-yellow plumes of the goldenrod offer a pleasant contrast.

Some shrubs bloom in September, too. The small yellow flowers of the native witch hazel can be seen in the fall, along with the spikes of tiny white flowers of the fall-blooming viburnums. Both shrubs and wildflowers are doing now what their spring counterparts did earlier: blooming and making seeds for a new generation.

Those of us who enjoy observing the out-of-doors see these things as representing another new beginning. We know, of course, that winter will terminate this second spring as surely as summer put an end to the earlier one. But we also know that you still have a couple of pleasant months left before winter to observe and enjoy nature from your back door.

WILDLIFE PANTRIES

W HEN WE THINK OF ANIMALS STORING FOOD FOR THE WINTER, the first one to come to mind for most people is the fox or gray squirrel and the way it buries nuts. Fox and gray squirrels bury each nut separately. This activity often takes place in the front lawn or flower bed, where it's obvious to homeowner and passer-by alike.

The red squirrel, too, stores nuts for the winter. It may bury them or stash them in a tree, a nest or a convenient attic. These caches may be quite large, amounting to two or three grocery sacks full. Flying squirrels also make large food caches like this.

The familiar chipmunk is another larder stocker. The chipmunk actually digs a separate compartment off the main tunnel of its burrow and fills it with food.

The deer mouse will stash its winter food supply in an abandoned bird's nest, a hollow log or tree or, if it's moved into your home for the winter, in an old boot or a kitchen drawer. Piles of firewood are also favorite places for the deer mouse's food cache. The best story I've heard was about a child's rockinghorse stored in an attic. The hollow horse had a mouse-sized hole in it, and by the time the mouse was done putting seeds in it, it was significantly heavier than it had been and it rattled when it bounced on its springs.

Another animal people commonly think of in connection with storing food for the winter is the beaver, which prepares for winter by

jamming branches in the mud under the ice. This underwater larder eliminates the need to risk coming out on the ice or the shore in the winter to feed.

A lot of the members of the weasel family make food caches, though they're temporary rather than sufficient for overwintering. I received a call recently from a homeowner who found two dead squirrels, some dead mice and a dead bird in the backyard woodpile. The caller thought someone was playing a joke on him by putting road kills on his woodpile. The joker was likely a skunk. When food is abundant, a skunk can find or kill more than it can eat. Like weasels and minks, the skunk may cache the surplus in a handy woodpile or hollow tree. If you find a pile of small dead animals on the edge of your suburban or rural backyard, you can bet one of the members of the weasel family has been active there.

In the bird world, three birds that are familiar to most homeowners stash food: the nuthatch, the blue jay and the American crow.

The nuthatch stashes seeds and fruits in cracks and crevices. Sunflower seeds from the bird feeder stashed under the edges of shingles are common signs of the nuthatch at work.

The blue jay will fill its throat sack full of sunflower seeds, then fly off in search of a place to hide the food. A clump of sunflowers growing where none were planted by humans probably indicates a blue jay food stash that was never revisited. The jay also tucks acorns away in the ground.

Crows will do basically the same thing, except the crows eat and cache a wide variety of foods. You're less likely to see the food-stashing behavior of crows, of course, because they tend not to be backyard birds.

Though fable and myth attribute wisdom to the animals that put food away for lean times, the fact is that food storing is strictly an innate or instinctive behavior. Animals store food in relation to its abundance — the more there is, the more they store. Weather folklore attributes some significance to the quantity of nuts that squirrels put away for the winter. But squirrels' storing large quantities of nuts has more to do with the good growing season for nut trees than the severity of the winter to come.

If food is abundant and an animal has sufficient storage facilities,

it may continue the food stashing beyond all reason, storing far more than it could consume. The seeds in the rockinghorse are probably a good example of an animal that responded to available food and an ideal storage place by storing more than it could possibly use. In a situation like that, storing may go on until the food, the storage place or the animal is exhausted.

Not all wild animals store food externally, but most of them store food internally by putting on layers of fat during the summer to get them through the winter.

Human beings tend to be the exception to the rule on food storage being a universal characteristic. Most of us don't stock the larder with an entire winter's food supply — we count on the food industry to do that for us. And we tend to put on weight during the winter and lose weight in the summer. You could say that's an illustration of just how far out of synch we are with the seasonal rhythms we observe in nature from your back door.

SYMBOLS OF THE SEASON

As THE HOLIDAYS APPROACH AND THE CHRISTMAS CARDS BEGIN to trickle in, it's obvious that a favorite image on these cards is birds.

One of the most frequently seen is the cardinal. Originally a bird of the southeastern United States, the cardinal has moved steadily northward over the past 100 years. Now it's common throughout much of Michigan and New England, and it has been adopted by most Easterners as a symbol of the season, probably because the rich Christmas red color of the male cardinal is so striking against the backdrop of white snow and dark evergreens in our yards.

Another bird that you see frequently on Christmas cards is the chickadee. One or more of seven species of chickadees occur almost everywhere in the United States. Consequently, most Americans can see and hear chickadees at Christmas time even in the depth of a northern winter. We interpret their energetic, bouncy movements and the call of "chicka-dee-dee-dee" as indicators that the chickadee is a friendly, happy, enthusiastic little bird. That's probably why we feature it on our holiday greeting cards.

Two other birds seen frequently on Christmas cards are geese and swans. The probable reasons for their association with the holiday are different from those of the cardinal and the chickadee.

Geese and swans are often portrayed on cards as flying against a backdrop of sky where a bright star is shining. The fact that these birds

migrate clear across the continent and navigate by the stars parallels somewhat the journey of the three wise men.

Another connection is the timing of their migration. Residents of northern areas tend to think of geese as fall birds, because we see the majority of them passing through in October and November. Residents of more southerly parts of the country associate the arrival of these migratory birds with the beginning of the Christmas season. The same is true of swans, though they tend to pass through Michigan a little later — from mid-November to mid-December.

Another Christmas card bird is the dove. It appears on holiday greetings not because of its color or its biology, but because it has become a symbol of peace. Therefore, the dove— usually a European dove or domestic pigeon — is a popular greeting card motif.

This idea of associating living things with Christmas started long ago and certainly isn't unique to Michiganders or North Americans. In Central America, for instance, swallows are the Christmas birds. In Michigan, we associate large flocks of swallows dipping and swooping over the backyard and sitting along roadside utility wires with summer coming to an end, because their congregating into flocks in late August or early September signals that they are preparing to head south. To residents of Belize and other Central American countries, however, swallows are the Christmas birds because they arrive there around the holiday season.

It's interesting that being aware of nature has resulted in natural objects or events taking a holiday role. Making such associations seems to be a fairly universal occurrence. Frequently, they transcend borders and even continents. We in North America, for instance, have within the past 50 years adopted the winter-blooming poinsettia of Mexico and Central America as a Christmas symbol. I seriously doubt, though, that swallows will ever displace our native cardinals and chickadees or migratory geese and swans on our Christmas greetings. Our Christmas birds will probably continue to be those you can see as you observe nature from your back door.

WINTER WEATHER AND WILDLIFE

WHEN FREEZING RAIN TURNS THE LANDSCAPE INTO ONE BIG SKATING pond, driving is hazardous and a trek to the mailbox becomes a test of skill and daring. It also makes life pretty difficult for many wild animals and birds.

Take the grouse, for instance. This bird feeds on tree buds, so snow generally doesn't affect its ability to find food. In fact, a thick blanket of snow for the grouse to snuggle into at night helps it withstand low temperatures and cold winter winds. An impervious layer of ice on top of the snow, however, can have one of two potentially disastrous effects: it can seal the grouse in (if the rain comes at night) or seal it out, leaving it without shelter. If conditions continue long enough, trapped birds may die of starvation. Birds on the surface may freeze.

Deer are hampered in their search for food by deep snow that makes it difficult or impossible for them to roam about. Deep snow with an ice crust on top of it is no improvement. When ice becomes thick enough to support the weight of dogs, coyotes and other predators, yet not thick enough to hold the deer, the deer become more vulnerable to predation and harassment.

Ground-feeding birds such as pheasant and quail can usually scratch through a loose snow or find wind-cleared patches of earth where they can feed. A coating of ice very effectively prevents these activities. Quail, particularly, are hard hit by severe cold and icy conditions.

For some animals, the icy roof on the snow is like armor that protects them against their enemies. Meadow mice, for instance, may get sleek and fat from feeding under the snow on seeds and the bark of fruit trees and ornamentals, while the animals that prey on them, such as foxes and hawks, are hungry and frustrated in their efforts to find food.

At other times, animals that feed on mice have an easy time of it. When there is very little snow cover, mice have to move about on the surface, where they are very vulnerable. When deep snow with an icy crust means mice are not available as a food source, foxes may hear them under the snow but be unable to get to them, and hawks must turn to other food sources. The red-tailed hawk and other large, soaring hawks, which feed primarily on rodents, must turn to larger mammals such as rabbits for food. There aren't nearly as many rabbits as there are mice, so the winter can be lean for big hawks.

A smaller hawk, the Cooper's hawk, is not as directly affected by snow because it feeds exclusively on smaller birds. As food gets harder to find, small birds may not have the energy supplies to escape from this agile hunter. People often make the pickings easier for the Cooper's hawk by feeding birds in their yards and so concentrating its food source. Lean times for this hawk tend to come in the spring, when bird numbers are down because of predation and winter mortality, and vegetation is greening up and providing the smaller birds with hiding places.

The animals that turn white in the winter are considerably

better off in a snowy year. When snow is scarce, the protective coloration of the snowshoe hare and the weasel is a distinct disadvantage — it makes them highly visible against the often bare ground. In snow, however, their white coats help them to be invisible right before your eyes.

To Michigan's hibernators, snow and ice are of no concern but temperature is critical. In a prolonged cold spell, the ground may freeze deep enough that these animals freeze to death.

Except for the thirteen-lined ground squirrel and the woodchuck, Michigan squirrels don't truly hibernate. They den up during severe weather but come out to forage for food during milder spells. Squirrels that bury nuts separately rather than store them in a cache in an attic or hollow tree can be cut off from their food supply by an icy crust. If lots of squirrels have buried nuts in the same general area, however, they may keep a hole open into the snow so they can get under the ice to dig up nuts.

Animals that stockpile food for the winter may get into trouble, too, as a result of the weather. Muskrats, for instance, pile up cattails in the fall and literally eat their way into the pile during the winter. As ice gets thicker, underwater food supplies get restricted and the muskrats are forced to eat more and more of their food stash.

Eventually, if the ice holds out longer than the muskrat food stashes, the animals may be forced out on the surface to feed in lawns, fields and meadows. This makes them very vulnerable to predators such as foxes and red-tailed hawks. After being cut off from their usual supply of mice, these predators are very prompt to take advantage of this new food source.

The fish that live in the muskrat pond may also be in trouble. A layer of snow over the ice cuts off the light that aquatic plants need to carry on photosynthesis. If they stop photosynthesizing, they quit producing the oxygen that the fish need to survive. The plants need a certain amount of oxygen, too, as well as sunlight. If they're deprived too long, they begin to die. The decomposition of the dead and dying plants uses up still more oxygen. Particularly in shallow lakes with lots of vegetation, the result can be a pond without a single living fish in it by spring.

Like wildlife, we humans are not immune to winter weather. It doesn't take much in the way of blowing snow or freezing rain to bring our cities to a slithering, sliding halt, either because our equipment fails or because we don't operate it properly. Then nature is no longer something we view from the security of our homes — it's a force we must contend with on a more intimate basis, and we may think of it as ugly and cruel. It is not ugly and cruel, however, nor beautiful and kind — it simply exists. If we can learn to work with it, not ignore it or needlessly destroy it or personify it, nature and an appreciation of it can greatly enrich our lives.

Chapter II
Wildlife Vignettes

THE GRAY TREE FROG

THERE'S A WILD CREATURE THAT YOU'RE JUST AS LIKELY TO encounter in a Detroit suburb as in the north woods. Chances are that you won't see it, however, and even if you did, you might not recognize it.

It's the gray tree frog. Over the years, I've had a lot of people ask the name of the animal that they can hear trilling day or night. Various people liken it to a cricket's song or the sound a baby raccoon makes or the call of a flicker (the large woodpecker with a white rump) — whichever sound they're familiar with.

The gray tree frog's trilling is high-pitched, unchanging in tone and loud, and its willingness to sing at any hour of the day or night from May throughout the whole summer means that people don't always find it an agreeable sound.

Often someone hearing the tree frog's trill will want to find out what's making the sound. Someone who hears it and mistakes it for something else may go rushing out to find the baby raccoon or woodpecker. Others don't care what's making the noise outside their bedroom windows — they just wish it wouldn't sing at 2 a.m.

It can be singing outside almost any bedroom window on a warm, humid, late spring or summer evening because the gray tree frog needs only trees and a spring pond to survive. Unlike the larger aquatic frogs, such as the bullfrog and leopard frog, the gray tree frog doesn't need a permanent body of water. A pond or ditch or small wetland that provides water from March through the end of summer is all it needs for reproduction. Any neighborhood that can provide water in the spring and trees can have a frog population.

Even though the gray tree frog is very common, it's rarely seen. For most people, their acquaintance with the gray tree frog remains an audible affair. The main reason they don't see the frog is that it can change its color to match that of its environment.

Like the much better known chameleon, the gray tree frog can turn charcoal gray, cement gray, apple green, blue-green, very pale yellow or brown, as well as mottled mixtures of these colors to blend into its surroundings. It is very effective camouflage.

It's too bad that it's stuck with such a dull name as gray tree frog. I've seen only one that was pure gray, and that's because it had climbed a chain link fence to catch insects drawn to a light. All the others I've seen over the years have been the color of tree bark, dirt or leaves or some combination of these — anything but gray!

It's also too bad that, even though it's a very common amphibian, very few people know of the color-changing tree frog. But there's hardly a school child that hasn't heard about the chameleon, even though true chameleons occur far away — around the Mediterranean and in Africa — and the tree frog is right in our backyards. (Anoles, which are frequently sold as chameleons, live in the southern United States and Central and South America.)

Maybe this says something about human nature and what

we value. If an animal or product comes from far away, it's somehow special and worthy of note. But if it's from right around home, it's nothing special to the point where it's ignored or even unknown.

Focusing on the nearby and the common, as we so often do in this column, can reveal some fascinating sights close to home, as well as some insights into ourselves, our attitudes and our values. The fascinating, the illuminating, even the unsettling are as close as nature from your back door.

OWLS

IF THERE'S EVER A CONTEST FOR MOST MISUNDERSTOOD TYPE of wildlife, owls will surely be in the running. The scientific information we have isn't nearly as abundant as the misinformation and superstitions about them.

One common misconception is that owls, particularly the great horned owl, are endangered, threatened or rare.

In Michigan, the barn owl is probably gone, but there's nothing rare about the great horned owl. It is common in rural areas and occasionally found in suburban and urban areas. It is abundant enough to be a nuisance, as anyone who has ever tried to raise ducks or chickens in a backyard pen without a cover on it can attest. One of the problems that biologists have had to consider in beginning to restore endangered peregrine falcons to certain areas of the state is predation by great horned owls.

Great horned owls and their smaller look-alike cousins the screech owls often frequent high school and college campuses. The combination of trees, shrubs and open, grassy areas that usually surround institutions like these are ideal habitat for the small mammals that owls prey on, and the owls take advantage of that food source. Several pairs of these "campus owls" reside on the

MSU campus, and most of the local high schools have at least a pair apiece. The owls are obviously not as common as starlings, but they are definitely not scarce.

One clue to how common they are is the frequency with which homeowners in rural and suburban areas get a whiff of skunk in their yards in the evening. The scent doesn't linger into the next day, however, as it would if the skunk had sprayed there, because the object of the skunk's attention had flown away. Great horned owls are one of the few predators that routinely dine on skunk. Because they have a poorly developed sense of smell, they don't let the skunk's potent defensive tactics deter them. They do often emerge smelling rather pungent, however, and they carry that scent around with them until it wears off.

Lots of people confuse the cooing of the mourning dove with the hooting of the great horned owl. True, they contain the same "oo" sound, but the dove's call is a soft, low, melodious but mournful sound, while the owl's is a series of hoots that starts and ends hard.

The great horned owl and its hooting are often connected with Halloween. But as a symbol of night and darkness, loneliness and spookiness, the great horned owl can't hold a candle to the barred owl. This owl of the swamps of northern Michigan is much better equipped to send chills down the spines of its audience.

Unlike the great horned owl, which has the tufts of feathers on its head that suggest ears and bright yellow eyes, the barred owl has no ear tufts and has dark eyes that look like black holes from a distance. Like the eyes of a shark, they look cold and dead.

Combined with the flat, dark face, the eyes give the barred owl a very baleful expression.

What really raises the hair on the back of your neck is to hear the barred owl's call at night.

The basic call is a series of eight hoots, higher pitched than those of the great horned owl, that supposedly sound like, "I'll cook for you, I'll cook for you, awww." It's a raucous, staccato call that falls and dies at the end. The owls can vary it tremendously by incorporating rising and falling notes that make it sound maniacal in the way of a loon's call or a hyena's laugh.

Imagine a harvest moon rising over a northern Michigan swamp with the mist beginning to collect and three or four of these owls getting into a hooting contest. It could be pretty spooky, even if you knew it was only owls. If it were up to me, it would be the barred owl on Halloween napkins, plates, cutouts and cards, not the great horned owl with his low hoot, a-hoot, hoot, hoot.

Owls are a good example of how the popular image of an animal may not bear much similarity to reality. The opportunity to observe wild animals and sort the truth out of the myth and misinformation is one of the neat things about studying nature from your back door.

BATS

To many people, August means warm summer nights, family picnics, back-to-school shopping, singing cicadas in the trees. To me, it means lots of calls about bats.

The reason is simple. August is the month that the young bats learn to fly and first follow their mothers outdoors to catch insects on the wing at night. Like all young things, they don't always get it right the first time. In leaving the roost where they were born and grew up, they are very likely to make a wrong turn or two. If the roost happens to be in someone's attic, the young bat ends up in the home's living quarters instead of the friendly skies. There it is likely to encounter very excited humans who waste no time and spare no effort to dispatch it.

This is unfortunate for the bat and can be very traumatic for the humans, who may encounter several bats in the course of a month. When they call me the question is invariably, "Why is my house being invaded by bats?"

The answer, of course, is that the bats have been there for some time. They may have moved into the house sometime in April or May or spent the winter in hibernation there. After mating, the males left and the females set up a maternity roost and started having young in June.

Bats don't live in the house in the same way that house mice

do — they merely sleep in it during the day, leaving at night to catch and eat flying insects. Their typical schedule is something like this: they leave shortly after sunset, return around the middle of the night to nurse their young for an hour or so, then leave again to feed some more, returning shortly before dawn to spend the daylight hours asleep.

Bats don't make nests. Their young are born on the rafters or in the eaves. Newborn young — they're about the size of a nickel — may cling to the female when she flies. When they reach the size of a quarter, she leaves them hanging on the rafters or under something stored in the attic when she goes out.

The calls about bats bumbling into living quarters usually start coming about mid-August. Sometimes I get bat calls at a rate of about two a day.

Most of the callers can't appreciate the uniqueness of the bat. It is the only true flying mammal ("flying" squirrels and other "flying" mammals are only gliders). Bats navigate by a biological type of sonar, sending out high-pitched sounds and listening for returning echoes to tell them about obstacles ahead. Because they feed exclusively on night-flying insects, bats are beneficial to human beings. They consume some of our least favorite insect pests, such as mosquitoes, moths, June bugs and other night-flying beetles.

Up close, a bat has a certain beauty. Its fur is very soft, almost like mole fur, and the membrane of its wings is like a very fine, very soft skin. The face — when the bat closes its mouth full of needle teeth — is more like that of a monkey or other primate than that of a rodent, dog or other long-nosed animal.

In spite of all that, you don't want bats in your house. Even a small number of bats will eventually make a smelly mess with their urine and droppings. And a large number will make enough noise to be annoying, especially when they're coming and going.

Most people don't want bats under their roof because they're terrified of bats. In many people's minds, the evil connotations associated with bats are all mixed up with two real fears: the fact that bats do occasionally have rabies, and the existence of vampire bats in other parts of the world. The result is a fright reaction all out of proportion to the threat the bats pose, which is limited at most.

The easy, permanent solution to bats in the house is to find the opening or openings they come and go through and seal them when the bats are out flying at night. That's all there is to it. If they can't find another way in, they'll roost elsewhere.

People often pass up the simple solution in favor of other methods that are more costly, take more time, pose some hazard to the people using them and aren't permanent. Why? I believe it's because climbing up and sealing a hole under the eaves doesn't provide the degree of satisfaction that people get from poisoning bats with toxic chemicals, zapping them with sonic devices or strewing the attic with pounds and pounds of mothballs. The simple solution is too simple, too ordinary — it somehow doesn't seem equal to the degree of fright that the bats provoke.

Sometimes people's fear of bats is so intense that they ask me how to get rid of the ones that flutter around the streetlights in their neighborhood at night or, in rural areas, around farmstead security lights.

Because August is bat month in Michigan, it seems too bad that Halloween comes at the end of October. Aug. 31 would be much more appropriate. After all, two of the wild animals we associate most with Halloween — bats and tree toads (more correctly called gray tree frogs) — are very common in August but nowhere to be seen in late October. Only owls are still around and very obvious, because they're at the peak of setting up their territories. Of the fluttering bats and chirping tree toads that are so common in late summer, however, there's not a sign.

To a person who appreciates backyard nature, two sure signs of warm summer days and nights are the bluebirds and the bats. Bat houses will probably never become as popular as bluebird houses, but bats can still be a manageable and interesting part of nature from your back door.

WEASELS

If you take even casual notice of the critters in your backyard, you've probably seen most of the animals we've talked about in this column. Some of the likely visitors to rural or suburban backyards you are very unlikely to see, however. One of those is the weasel.

Michigan's largest weasel, found throughout the state, is the long-tailed weasel, which reaches a length of about 10 inches. Its smaller cousin, found in the Upper Peninsula and northern lower Michigan, is the short-tailed weasel, or ermine, which measures about 8 inches. The least weasel, about 6 inches long, occurs throughout the southern part of the state.

For several good reasons, even though these animals may be frequent visitors to your backyard, it's unlikely that you'll see them.

First of all, weasels work the night shift. They do most of their moving around and hunting at night.

Second, they travel by slipping under, squeezing between and gliding over obstacles. Slender, agile animals, they most resemble a snake in the way they slink around your yard.

It's this mode of travel that's given rise to use of the term "weasel" to describe people who are slinky and devious and secretive, and "weasel out," meaning to sidestep or circumvent an obligation or situation. Likewise, a "weasel word" is one chosen to avoid making a direct or forthright statement.

Anyone who has seen a weasel on the hunt knows that evasion or avoidance of direct action is not the weasel's way when there's prey to be had. Weasels attack ferociously and fearlessly, and if cornered, they will put up a fierce defense.

A third reason that weasels can come and go unseen is their color. In the summer, their coats are a rich brown except for the underside from throat to pelvic area, which is a creamy yellow. As they move through tall grass and weave their way around shrubs in the dark, they blend right into the deep shadows. In the winter, they turn white except for the black tips of their tails. So, in a snowy winter, they are so well camouflaged that you are even less likely to see them then than in the summer.

Also, it's easy to confuse a large long-tailed weasel with a small mink, especially if you don't see the buff underbelly of the weasel. Mink, however, are larger and usually darker brown, and they have only a small white streak under the chin and on the throat.

Many people find out weasels are in the neighborhood when they try to raise poultry or rabbits in the backyard. A determined long-tailed weasel can kill an adult chicken or a rabbit, though either would be too big for it to drag away or consume entirely. The first sign that a weasel has visited the chickens, then, is likely to be a partially eaten carcass and a pile of feathers discovered one morning.

If you don't raise weasel food, your yard may still provide it in the form of mice, moles, ground squirrels and chipmunks. You may not know the weasels are there, however, unless you find paw prints in bare earth or snow, or unless the family dog or cat happens to catch a weasel or one gets caught in a mole trap. (Least weasels frequently run along mole tunnels to hunt the moles.)

In spite of the time I spend observing wildlife in my backyard, I have never seen a weasel there. I know they come visiting, however, because I've seen their tracks. I have also seen them run across the road at night, and I've encountered them in forest and field.

It's too bad that we don't see the weasel more often. But perhaps its secretive nature is part of our fascination with it. Except when it's killing small livestock, it's basically on our side in the continuing battle against rats and mice. People with backyard chickens and rabbits who eliminate the weasels that take an occasional chicken often find out that the rats take up where the weasels left off, and in greater numbers, thanks to the elimination of a voracious predator.

A better strategy would be to weasel-proof the chicken or rabbit quarters with sheet metal or hardware cloth as needed to prevent weasels from digging, climbing or chewing their way in. This will also keep the rats out and help discourage larger predators such as dogs, foxes, raccoons, skunks and domestic cats. And it will help to maintain an amiable relationship between you and wildlife, which is a basic part of enjoying nature from your back door.

Chapter III

Animal Behavior

ANIMAL INTELLIGENCE

Usually this column deals with backyard nature topics that tend not to make national headlines.

But I had an experience recently that made me wonder about something that had been the topic of a Newsweek cover story, namely, just how smart are animals, anyway?

My train of thought began on Memorial Day weekend as I was watering some pansies in a windowbox. A female robin flew down and landed about 8 feet away and then just stood there and looked at me. I wondered aloud why the robin was behaving that way, and my wife informed me it was obvious that the robin wanted a drink.

Though I thought she was jumping to a conclusion on the basis of very little evidence, I obligingly turned the hose toward the robin.

She didn't get a drink — she just stood there and watched the water fall all around her. It surprised me that she didn't fly away as soon as I turned toward her, or at least when the water began to hit her. Eventually, she began pecking at the ground.

I didn't think the water could have been falling on the soil long enough to bring up insects or earthworms for the robin to eat, so I kept watching. It soon became obvious that she was collecting mud in her beak. When she had accumulated a big dollop of it, she flew back to her nest in a nearby walnut tree and lined her nest with it.

My wife had been right in her conclusion that the robin wanted something. What impressed me was that the robin appeared to have been standing there waiting for me to make mud.

For starters, I had not been spraying water from the hose over a large area, but rather trickling it inconspicuously into the windowbox. So how could the robin associate what I was doing with the hose with water, let alone the manufacture of mud?

That brought up the whole question of animal intelligence and the difficulty in distinguishing learned associations — such as human plus hose equals water plus lawn equals mud — and conclusions reached by reasoning.

We know animals can learn by association, so it's not phenomenal that an older, experienced bird (which this one obviously was) could have made the association between humans, hoses and water. But for her to stand there in front of me waiting for me to turn the hose on the ground and make mud for her would seem to require some reasoning. "If I go down there and stand, he will make mud for me to line my nest."

What's more likely, of course, is that the robin has gathered mud in watered lawns before and had made the association between hoses, water, lawns and mud. The fact that the robin didn't fly off when I turned the hose toward her suggests it must have been a very strong association, a very well learned behavior, if it could override her instinctive response to possible danger.

I arrived at that explanation of the robin's behavior after a

fairly long process of observation and reasoning. I still can't explain how my wife knew intuitively that the robin wanted something.

"It's easy for one mother to recognize another mother in need," was her explanation.

The implications of that statement are much more than I want to deal with in this column! I'll leave it to the researchers on left brain, right brain functions to determine how men and women take such radically different routes to the same conclusions, and I'll stick with safer topics, such as animal intelligence and manifest-ations of it in nature from your back door.

STRANGE ANIMAL BEHAVIOR

A LOT OF THE WAYS THAT ANIMALS BEHAVE ARE BUILT INTO them. When the stimuli are right, the animals perform certain behaviors whether they seem appropriate or not.

In most cases, we see these inappropriate behaviors in birds.

The most common, which we have probably all either seen or read about, occurs when a bird has set up a nesting territory that it defends against other birds, especially those of the same species. If that territory includes a window or other reflective surface, such as a polished car bumper or hubcap, the bird sees its image and tries to chase it away. The observer sees a bird crashing again and again into the window or chrome and may assume that the bird is attacking it or, in the case of the window, trying to break through it and into the house.

This sort of behavior can be puzzling or, especially to fans of Alfred Hitchcock movies, even frightening. Even if you understand what's going on, it may still be quite disturbing. The bird may begin its attack shortly after sunrise and continue most of the day — or until it's too exhausted or injured to go on.

The bird simply can not understand that the other bird it sees is not an intruder. All it can do is react according to its instinct.

Nest building behavior may also go astray occasionally, especially among robins. If the female robin has an abundance of nest materials and suitable sites for nests, she may start several nests in various spots before she finally finishes one and settles down in it. A porch with several columns, for instance, might have the beginnings of a nest on the top of each column. A ladder may have a nest on each step, all built by the same bird that is responding to the abundance of materials and sites in the only way she is able.

After nest building comes egg laying, and people are often surprised to find unbroken eggs lying far from any nest. The first thought is that somehow the eggs fell out of a nest, but it's more likely that the female birds laid them right where they were found.

Once they're in egg production, female birds lay an egg a day. During this time, a female will have several eggs inside her in various stages of development. Once an egg gets to a certain point in the process, it can not be reabsorbed but must finish developing and be laid — somewhere.

If the nest is destroyed, the bird will have nowhere to put her egg. She can't reverse the process, however, or put it on hold while she rebuilds her old nest or builds a new one. So she puts the egg down wherever she happens to be when it's time to lay it, no matter whether that's in the middle of your lawn or on top of a fence post.

Sometimes a bird ready to lay an egg will see a nest with other eggs in it and put hers there, too. These so-called "dump nests" may have as many as 20 or more eggs in them. Wood ducks are known for this behavior. One wood duck female may find herself sitting on 15 or 20 eggs, some hers, some belonging to passers-by. Because the eggs are in her nest, the wood duck tries to incubate them and raise the hatchlings.

As birds raise their young, observers are sometimes puzzled by the parent's failure to try to care for a young bird that's fallen out of the nest. If the baby bird was not yet ready to leave the nest, the parents ignore it because it has no meaning to them once it's out of the nest. What they respond to is the presence of the babies in the nest. Babies not in the nest that they built are simply not theirs.

Once the babies are ready to fly out of the nest, however, the nest loses its meaning and the parents recognize the young as individuals and will feed them wherever they happen to be. That's when you'll see some hulking youngster hopping along behind its parent begging for food, even though it's as large or larger than the adult and looks perfectly capable of feeding itself. If the parent bird drops the food, the youngster will direct its begging behavior at the food, as if that will make the food jump into its mouth. It takes a while for the young ones to make the transition from being fed to picking up food and eating it.

If your lawn has trees and shrubs that attract birds, you're likely to see at least some of these behaviors sooner or later. If you understand a little about why they occur, they aren't quite so incomprehensible, even though they are still inappropriate. Recognizing them for behaviors gone amiss will enrich both your understanding and your enjoyment of nature from your back door.

NESTING BEHAVIOR

LAST TIME WE TALKED ABOUT SOME OF THE ODD NESTING behavior we see in birds in the backyard. In this column we're going to follow up on that and talk about the various ways birds raise their young.

One of these ways is exemplified by the killdeer.

Most of us have probably noticed killdeer on playgrounds, schoolyards and other open, grassy areas. The adults are very noticeable birds. Slightly larger than a robin, they have a white breast with two black bands across the front at the top, a brown back, white underwings and a piercing call that is supposed to sound like "kill-deer."

The killdeer lays eggs in a shallow depression on the ground. The eggs and the young birds are so well camouflaged that even a trained observer can look right at them without seeing them.

As soon as the young dry off after hatching, they can follow their parents around. In this way, the killdeer are like pheasants and chickens. The parents lead the chicks to food and water and away from predators. We don't often see the young even then, however, because if we get too close to the young, the parents try to distract us by running around, calling and, if necessary, performing a very convincing fluttering, twittering, broken wing routine to lure us away from the young. The babies, in the meantime, have flattened themselves against the ground and lain very still, letting their camouflage coloring conceal them.

The young, which usually hatch in May and June, are ready to fly with their parents in July.

In the other type of young-rearing approach, as demonstrated by robins and starlings, the young stay in the nest until they are ready to fly and the parents bring food and feed them. After they come off the nest and can fly to some degree, their basic strategy is just the opposite of that of the killdeer. The young sit on the ground or in shrubs while the parents go out and forage. While they wait, the young give a special food begging call. When they see or hear the adult, their begging becomes louder, more persistent and very obvious. Then the parents feed them.

The killdeer young are mobile but try to stay out of sight. The young of the starling or robin are noisy and make themselves as obvious as possible so their parents will feed them. We rarely see the killdeer but frequently encounter young starlings and robins alone because their parents are out looking for food. As these young become stronger flyers, they, too, follow their parents around, though they still expect to be fed. Killdeer young, on the other hand, pick at food that their parents have led them to. Young starlings and robins have to learn to pick up food for themselves and may be seen begging at the food, as well as the parents, as if they think it will jump into their mouths.

In both types of birds, the young watch the adults, learning to do what they do, to avoid what they avoid, and to learn what they need to do to survive. The fact that their strategies for survival vary from species to species is one of the things that make it so interesting to observe nature from your back door.

PLAYING POSSUM

WHEN WARM WEATHER IN JANUARY BRINGS BATS AND SNAKES temporarily out of hibernation to horrify homeowners, another animal is also out and about under the influence of the mild weather: the opossum.

The opossum (or possum, as you'll more often hear it called) is North America's only marsupial — it carries its young in a pouch as a kangaroo does. It's a southern mammal that's relatively new to most of Michigan. It became abundant in southern Michigan about a hundred years ago, and only in the past 50 years or so has it become common in northern Michigan.

To get through severe cold, it becomes inactive and sleeps a lot. It's not a true hibernator, like the groundhog — it just holes up when the weather gets bad. Then, when a mild period comes along, the opossum leaves its hollow log or protected nook under a wooden deck or mobile home and scurries out to look for something to eat. Unseasonably mild weather in January and early February brings possums out in full force.

When this happens, I receive numerous calls about possums, usually from people who are alarmed at the sight of what looks like a big rat with a mouthful of needlelike teeth. They worry that it will harm their children or pets. During one midwinter thaw, I even saw a couple of possums as far north as Cheboygan County. The one that I'll remember for a long time, however, is the one I met "up close and personal" in my backyard on a mild January night.

Late one evening as I was about to turn out the lights, I noticed a possum cleaning up seed under a bird feeder close to a large picture window. When it saw me at the window, it struck a ferocious pose with head up, mouth open, saliva dripping from all 50 of its sharp teeth, and one paw upraised. Thinking that here was one possum that wasn't going to play dead, I went about my business. When I came back a few minutes later, it was still in that ferocious pose.

My previous experience with possums included some that played possum and a few that didn't, some that would bite if you tried to grab them and some that remained motionless no matter what happened to them. But I had never before seen one playing possum standing up.

Figuring that it was hungry, I took it a piece of bread. It held its fierce pose as I walked up to it and impaled the bread on its lower canine teeth. It still didn't move—it just stood there, with that ferocious look on its face and a piece of bread hanging from its mouth.

Finally, 17 minutes after it froze, it literally snapped out of its trance, as if it had been hit with a jolt of electric current. Its head snapped around and the jaws snapped shut on the bread, biting a piece out. Both pieces of bread fell and the possum whirled away and ran into the darkness.

Besides demonstrating that the possum is not one of our most fearsome mammals, this tale seems to back up the claim by

physiologists that the possum does not have voluntary control over the state that it is in when it's playing possum. It is evidently locked in for a period of time until whatever physiological mechanism that sent it into that state releases it.

It's hard to imagine that this arrangement for faking death could have much survival value if the possums can't end the act at will. It may last only moments or hours. Or the game may become reality if, during that time when the possum is immobilized, some possum predator happens along and discovers an easy meal waiting for it.

All of our larger predators — bears, coyotes, foxes, bobcats, great horned owls, red-tailed hawks — will eat possums when the opportunity arises. The possum has still managed to become increasingly abundant in our state, so playing possum must help it survive, or at least not be too detrimental. Playing possum in front of an oncoming Ford, Chevrolet or Plymouth is obviously futile, but maybe no more so than trying to dodge out of the way.

The story of my backyard possum shows that animals just being themselves are often funnier than cartoonists can make them by turning them into little people. (Just think: if that possum hadn't had a firm base of support from three legs and a tail, he might have tipped over when he went into his act.) Dramatic, thought-provoking, amazing and funny —- yes, humor, too, is part of nature from your back door.

BIG GAME IN THE BACKYARD

WHEN MOST OF US THINK OF BACKYARD WILDLIFE, WE TEND TO think of small animals such as squirrels, rabbits, robins and cardinals. If we live near water, we might add ducks and geese to the list. But most of us — in southern lower Michigan, at least — wouldn't ordinarily think of large animals in the backyard, such as bears, bobcats or deer.

But for suburban and rural residents in southern Michigan, having deer in the backyard is becoming as commonplace as it is for residents of northern lower Michigan and the U.P.

Deer frequent these yards because of the food they can find there and, during the firearm deer season, for sanctuary from hunters.

Backyards offer fallen apples and pears, crabapples, vegetable garden leftovers, seed in bird feeders, and tender twigs of ornamental trees and shrubs. Deer seem to be especially fond of arborvitae and members of the apple family and other fruit trees. In my backyard, the earth under the apple trees toward the back of the yard is crisscrossed with the tracks of deer that have come into the yard to clean up fallen fruits.

During hunting season, deer may use rural and suburban yards as a refuge from hunters. When disturbed and driven out of their usual haunts, deer will move into other areas where they are less likely to be disturbed. They may not stay long in a suburban backyard — maybe just for that part of the day when hunters are most active — or they may bed down there and stay until disturbed by dogs or playing children. A yard with a thick stand of shrubs or a brush-lined creek running through the back of it may provide both food and shelter.

The deer that benefit from this survival strategy are those that have learned to tolerate being around human habitations without panic. When hunting activity becomes frequent, they will move quietly into a backyard thicket, a small wetland between two lawns or an overgrown drainage ditch because they have learned that they won't be disturbed there.

Most hunters who have hunted woodland or cropland on the suburban fringe will have stories to tell of seeing deer jump out of backyards when they are returning from the hunt or hearing stay-at-home spouses or neighbors tell of the big buck that strolled through the yard just after they left.

Sometimes deer seeking refuge in residential areas can't handle being so close to humans and they panic. Spooked this way and then that, they end up running through plate glass windows or out in front of cars in busy downtown areas. The only deer I have ever hit with my car came out of a backyard on the edge of Grand Ledge, after I had stopped watching for deer because we were practically in town.

Deer in the yard are becoming more common, particularly in suburban counties where a lot of former agricultural land is sitting idle between rural subdivisions or where undeveloped flood plains of rivers provide travel lanes from one undeveloped tract to another. Some cities where this occurs include Grand Rapids, Kalamazoo, Midland, and Sterling Heights, Farmington Hills, Bloomfield Hills and other cities in the Detroit metropolitan area.

Some rural and suburban residents set out to attract deer into their yards regularly by feeding them. Others are less than happy to see deer or deer tracks in their yards because of the damage deer can do to landscape ornamentals and gardens.

Having deer in your yard, then, can certainly be a mixed blessing. But as long as the deer are temporary visitors and any injury they might cause can either be prevented or ignored (because plants will outgrow it), most people would probably agree that seeing them up close can be one of the more spectacular experiences in observing nature from your back door.

Chapter IV

When Wildlife Cause Problems

DUCKS IN CHIMNEYS
AND OTHER UNUSUAL PROBLEMS

ORDINARILY, I TRY TO DESCRIBE WILDLIFE EXPERIENCES THAT most people encounter sooner or later, but this time I want to describe some of the more unusual experiences that illustrate how fascinating and diverse nature from your back door can be. We can also learn some basic wildlife principles from these rare encounters.

The first story to come to mind began when someone called to report there was a duck stuck in their chimney. Now, a duck in the chimney sounds pretty unlikely unless you are familiar with the wood duck. It nests in cavities in trees along rivers and streams. Presumably the duck we pulled out of the chimney flue had been investigating what she thought was a likely-looking cavity when she fell in. For her, it was a one-way trip. For us, it was a sooty lesson in wood duck biology.

Another year, someone called to tell me they thought they had a rattlesnake in their chimney. Considering the scarcity of rattlesnakes in Michigan, and the fact that rattlesnakes just don't climb on houses, that's very unlikely. But the sound coming out of the chimney did sound like the buzz of a rattler's rattle. When we opened the flue — ver-r-r-ry carefully — out fell a nest of baby chimney swifts.

Usually the chimney swift's nest stays stuck to the inner wall of the chimney. A windstorm can create a strong downdraft that blows it loose, however. The adult chimney swift can flutter up and down the chimney shaft, but the young birds cannot. The sound they make when they beg for food is a kind of buzzing — something like the rattle of a rattlesnake. Before the advent of chimneys, the swift nested in hollow trees. Today, in the forest of chimneys in urban areas, the chimney swift is a familiar urban and suburban resident.

Both these stories, though they are amusing, illustrate the importance of putting a screen over the chimney to keep the critters out. A squirrel or starling that falls in, gets into the house, and tracks or flaps soot all over the walls, drapes and furniture is not so amusing. As with people, "fences" make good wildlife neighbors.

Even in a city like Lansing, "Guess who's coming to dinner?" sometimes has some unusual answers. It's not uncommon for families to feed raccoons or squirrels. The animals learn to come at regular mealtimes. Squirrels may even learn to rattle a screen door to get someone's attention. Sometime in June or July, the female raccoons may start bringing their young with them to participate in the meal.

Ducks, geese and gulls that share a lake with people often become so accustomed to people, especially if someone feeds them, that they become regular tenants of boat docks, decks, yards, swimming pools and patios. Occasionally, ducks nest inside the fence around a pool and need help in getting the ducklings out of the pool and into the lake or river.

Unfortunately, not all neighbors regard these wildlife boarders with enthusiasm. For some people, these wild creatures are noisy, messy, obtrusive pests, much like human in-laws that long overstay their welcome.

Severe weather sometimes produces some unusual relationships. In extremely cold weather chickadees may roost in a garage. In an unseasonably cold spring, a homeowner may find his bluebird house stuffed with bluebirds huddled to keep warm. In winter, Cooper's hawks may visit backyard bird feeders, not to eat the bird seed, but to eat the birds that eat the seed. When this happens, some people understand and appreciate the ecological relationships among the weather, the feeder, the seed-eating birds and the hawk. Others just see a killer.

Occasionally the actions of some wild animals pose a puzzling mystery. Imagine awakening one morning to find that one of your large potted plants had been unpotted in the night. Or suppose you opened the drawer where you keep the dish towels, removed one and found, neatly arranged, five nuts from the Christmas bowl. Your first thought might be that someone in the family was up to mischief or practical joking. But the culprits are a shrew and a deer mouse.

Shrews scratch through the soil looking for insects. If they wander into a house, the only soil available is in the potted plants. Deer mice make caches of food collected elsewhere. Nuts, dry dog food and sunflower seeds from the bird feeder may turn up almost anywhere.

Because both these animals are secretive and mostly nocturnal, their presence often goes undetected until the mysterious occurrences give them away. Until they are understood, however, the neat, unpredictable and unexplained food caches of deer mice have led some people to doubt their families or their own sanity.

WILD GUESTS MAY WEAR OUT THEIR WELCOME

JUNE IS OFTEN "I TOLD YOU SO" MONTH FOR WILDLIFE BIOLOGISTS. It is the time when people who did not listen to advice not to encourage swans and Canada geese to hang around their yards begin to find out why that advice was given.

Earlier, people who live near water enjoyed seeing pairs of Canada geese or mute swans swimming together in their dignified, stately manner. They may have even witnessed the birds' courtship rituals. Canada geese come breast to breast and rear up out of the water and beat their wings. Swans come breast to breast and arch their necks and touch their heads together, forming a heart shape. Though the birds may have come near people and accepted food offered to them, they generally kept a discreet distance and retired with dignity to a secluded area when people approached too near. In short, they were ideal wildlife guests.

After courtship comes mating and then nesting and the arrival of the young birds. Geese usually do not cause any problems in nesting, but swans may by choosing to nest on someone's patio or back porch. Mute swans are domesticated birds from Europe that are living semi-wild in Michigan, and you never know where they may decide to nest.

Conflicts between humans and birds often begin after the eggs hatch. The males defend their broods and can deliver painful blows with the bony front edges of their wings. If you are not expecting this change, you may feel betrayed. After all, you fed these animals and allowed them to homestead on your property, and look how they are returning your good will! Instead of quietly moving away when you approach, the adults, especially the males, may turn on you and attack, instinctively protecting their young, even though you mean no harm.

That is not the worst of it, however.

In the next month, the half-dozen or so young birds will grow very quickly, approximating the size of the adults. As part of their diet, these birds consume grass, and because they grow so quickly, they must eat a lot of grass.

As they eat a lot of grass, they also produce a lot of waste. Where you once had two animals spending a little time on your property, you now have eight or so spending a lot of time there, eating the grass and defecating on the lawn, on the beach and in the water.

That may not be the worst, either. This family flock may attract other family flocks so that, by the end of the summer, your original pair may have grown to number dozens or even hundreds of birds with the accompanying mess of feathers and feces.

The best way to deal with this problem is not to encourage that original pair to feel at home. Resist the temptation to provide food for them. Treat them like any other wild animal and keep them at a distance where you can enjoy them without coming into conflict with them. If necessary, take active measures to repel them or even drive them off. When geese first arrive, build a fence of 18-inch high stakes and string and/or strips of bird scare foil between the nearby lake or pond and your lawn. Geese cannot or will not cross string, especially in the summer when young are too small to fly and adults have molted. If fencing is not feasible, get a permit from the DNR and harass the geese — with spray from a garden hose, a broom, firecrackers, etc. — whenever they venture onto the lawn. Let them be your neighbors, but keep them at a distance. Then, instead of a major nuisance or even a danger, they can be just another delightful part of nature from your back door.

DR. JEKYLL AND MR. GULL

THE WHITE BODY, GRAY WINGS AND BLACK WING TIPS OF THE seagull are familiar to most of us. For many people, seeing a gull or hearing its familiar cry brings to mind pleasant images of blue water, blue sky and sunny vacations by the shore.

People who live with gulls all the time, however, may see another side of this handsome bird. And people who see gulls only now and again under a variety of circumstances may find them a source of confusion.

The confusion begins with the seagull's name. These attractive gray and white birds are found around the Great Lakes, near inland lakes and ponds, in city playgrounds and shopping mall parking lots, and in freshly plowed fields far from any lake. Gulls they are — but not necessarily seagulls.

Obviously gulls are extremely adaptable. Though they are true water birds, they are quite at home on land. Though we think of them as fish eaters, they will also eat worms and insects, fruits and fleshy vegetables, garbage, and scraps from a backyard cookout or picnic in the park.

Adults of the several species of gulls that live in Michigan look very much alike. The young, however, tend to look less like their parents than their parents look like other kinds of adult gulls. Young ringbill gulls, for example, have a pink bill and legs and plumage mottled in gray, brown and white the first year. Only after three years do these birds develop the adult's yellow bill with a black ring around it, yellow legs and snow-white head and breast, gray wings and black wing tips.

The ringbill is about the size of a crow, so people who are familiar with it have that impression of the appropriate size for a gull. When they first encounter the herring gull, which is the size of a mallard duck or bigger but is superficially the ringbill's twin, they become confused just as I first did. "I had no idea gulls were so big!" is a typical comment.

Another gull moving into Michigan from the north is even bigger than the herring gull. The great black-backed gull is so dark on its wings that it looks black. This gull and Bonaparte's gull, which has a jet-black head, are easy to recognize as adults, but except for size, their young and the young of other gulls can be quite confusing.

Becoming familiar with the habits of the gulls may further alter an idealized image of the gull.

Though we think of gulls as fish eaters, we tend to think of them swooping down to snatch live fish from the waves rather than scavenging dead fish on the beach. Gulls, however, play an important role in cleaning up dead or injured and dying fish in the lake and on the shore. They will scavenge garbage, too, as well as leftover fish bait.

They are also predators that prey on smaller birds. When gulls prey on newly hatched ducklings, goslings or cygnets where viewing these waterfowl is a local attraction, the white-wings-soaring-against-the blue-sky image that so many people have of gulls often has to be revised.

White-droppings-on-the-dock is a more down-to-earth problem that lakeshore dwellers often have to deal with. The droppings are abundant and, because much of the gull's diet consists of fish, very smelly. Gulls can make a slippery, smelly mess of any boat, pier, dock or raft on which they roost. In places like the locks at Sault Ste. Marie, gull droppings on catwalks pose a hazard to lock operators and engineers. When the droppings dry and oxidize, they become corrosive and can damage metal, wood finishes and cloth.

All this is not to suggest that gulls are devils rather than saints. It simply shows that they are adaptable, complex birds doing what they can to make a living. Sometimes that puts them in conflict with people. Sometimes people react more strongly to their problems with gulls if they once held the Jonathan Livingston Seagull image of the soaring white birds and find that image betrayed by reality.

Sometimes giving up such notions is part of the study of nature from your back door.

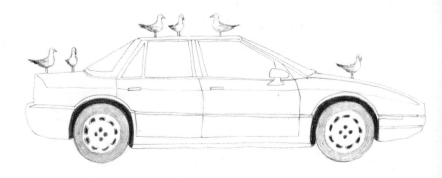

ENCOUNTERS WITH SKUNKS

THERE IS AN ANIMAL THAT IS COMMON IN MOST NEIGHBORHOODS throughout Michigan. At the same time it is so unobtrusive — usually — that it can live undetected literally under a homeowner's nose. It's nocturnal, so we normally do not see it. It makes its presence known only when it is disturbed by another animal or human or when its feeding in the lawn or garden creates a problem.

It's been dubbed "the most feared mammal on the North American continent," not because of its ferocity or size or strength, but because of what it carries under its tail. You guessed it: it's the skunk.

In Michigan, it's the striped skunk, though that name can be misleading. Striped skunks may have no white on them at all, the classic white cap and/or two full-length or partial white stripes, or some other variation of the black and white theme. One thing is certain: when they let loose their olfactory calling card, they can't be mistaken for anything else.

Skunks often come into conflict with humans when they choose to make their den under a house with a crawl space, a porch or deck, a mobile home or a portable classroom. The occupants of these structures may live on top of a skunk for some time without knowing it's there because the skunk itself doesn't stink — it has an animal odor just as a horse or a dog does, but it doesn't smell like what it sprays. People find out that the animal is there when something else gets under the structure or alarms the skunk out in the open and it defends itself.

On many occasions, I have been called into situations involving a skunk living under a structure and with a box trap caught raccoons, possums, cats and rats but no skunks. Tracks and the distinctive signs of skunks' digging show that the skunk is still present, but the skunk problem — the odor — disappears because I removed the animals that provoked the skunk to spray.

Another problem with skunks is damage to the lawn as they dig for grubs and damage to the garden as they forage in the sweet corn, tomatoes and cantaloupe.

Skunks have mitt-like front paws with big claws for digging. With one or two swipes, they can open and push aside the sod and dig down 2 to 3 inches where the grubs are. A busy skunk can make a lawn look as if a mad golfer has been rampaging around the lawn making divots.

Damage in the garden is less distinctive. Woodchucks, raccoons, deer and, in urban areas, rats will also feed in the garden at night. Tracks in garden soil or sightings of the intruders at work may be necessary to determine what animal is involved.

People who keep chickens or ducks may find out that skunks are fairly effective predators when their prey cannot get away from them. A big skunk can handle an adult chicken or duck, though a goose is too much for it. Chicks and ducklings, of course, are easy prey.

Often we learn that a skunk is nearby in a most traumatic fashion. The script goes something like this: the family is ready for bed and somebody lets the dog out one last time before everybody settles down for the night. After a few moments of furious barking, the dog scratches on the door to come in. Realization dawns when somebody opens the door and smells skunk, but the hysterical dog is faster than the door opener's reflexes and it's inside and bolting to its favorite safe retreat — under the bed, behind the sofa, wherever — before anyone can stop it. The dog's coat is saturated with the smelly oil from the skunk, and it leaves liberal doses of it on rugs, upholstery, bedclothes, the clothing of family members trying to head it off and get it outside, and everything else it touches. The pungent stuff is very irritating to the eyes and nasal passages, and if the dog received the spray directly in the face at short range, it may have suffered permanent eye damage.

An encounter I had with a skunk trapped in an elevator shaft taught me that getting the skunk odor out of clothing and other portable fabrics — that is, things you can take outside to air — isn't that big a deal. After airing and perhaps being rained on or rinsed once or twice, clothes can be washed in a strong detergent without stinking up the whole house. For upholstery and rugs that have to stay in place, at least two skunk-neutralizing products are available commercially. You will usually find them among the grooming aids in horse and dog supply catalogs. Your local veterinarian or pet store operator may also have them or know where you can get them. In the meantime, acetic acid — in the form of vinegar or tomato juice — followed by a good scrubbing with a shampoo for oily hair should make your dog fit to live with again, though he still may smell a little skunky, especially when he gets wet.

After an encounter with a skunk, people often want to know

NATURE FROM YOUR BACK DOOR

how they can get rid of the skunk, meaning exterminate it. Because skunks feed on nests of baby mice and rabbits, ground-nesting wasps and bees, and moles, getting rid of the skunks just because they're in the neighborhood might simply be trading one problem for another one.

Don't assume you have a skunk problem just because you get a whiff of skunk odor in the yard. If it's gone the next morning, you may have smelled a great horned owl reeking of skunk. These large owls prey on skunks and don't seem to mind the odor.

When a skunk is under the house or somewhere else where it is likely to be provoked frequently, however, you do have to do something about it.

One thing that will not work is sealing up the entry to the den it has dug. Skunks are very powerful diggers. If you fill the entrance with dirt and cement blocks, the skunk will simply move over a couple of feet and dig a new entrance. The only solution is to catch the skunk in either a trap that kills instantly or a box trap, and then kill it or release it some distance away. Then you need to install some partially buried L-shaped skirting to prevent some other skunk from moving in.

Where do backyard skunks come from? They're around all along. The amazing thing is not that they make their presence known in such a dramatic and unmistakable manner, but that they go undetected for so long. Knowing that the skunk has probably been around for some time, and that there are doubtless others in the vicinity can make you aware of the potential problems so you can prevent them, avoid an odoriferous conflict and continue to enjoy observing nature from your back door.

Chapter V

Nature as Teacher

A CHANCE TO LEARN
FROM THE BIRDS

B IRD FEEDING IS AN OPPORTUNITY TO GET SOME ECOLOGICAL insights into backyard wildlife.

A basic ecological concept is the idea of niche, the way an animal makes use of its habitat to survive. We are recognizing this when we put out different foods for different birds. The sunflower seeds, cracked corn, millet, thistle seeds, peanut butter, suet, and bits of apple and orange in our feeders appeal to a variety of birds that live in the same habitat. If you know whether a particular bird is a seed eater or an insect eater, you can put out food tailored to its food preferences. Or you can put out a varied mixture and observe which birds feed on what.

You will also observe that various birds obtain the same food in different ways. Sunflower seeds are a good example. A number of bird species eat sunflower seeds, but how the birds solve the problem of getting the kernel from the shell varies from species to species.

The larger finches, including the cardinal, squeeze the seeds in their beaks until the hard shells pop open. The grosbeaks are the masters of this technique, snapping and gulping seeds in rapid succession. The goldfinch has to work a bit harder. Its beak is not as large, so it has to get just the right angle on the seed to pop it open.

Chickadees are among the species that pound the seeds open. A chickadee will hold a seed between its feet and then pound on it with its beak to crack it. Often you'll see a chickadee pound a hole in a seed, eat what it can reach through that hole and then pound another one. The tufted titmouse also takes this approach.

The nuthatch likes sunflower seeds but isn't equipped with a beak for squeezing them or feet for holding them while it pounds them open. To crack the hard shell, it must find something else to hold the seed. A crevice in the bark of a tree, in a piece of weathered barn wood or under a shingle on the side of your home works just fine.

The blue jay also carries seeds away to eat them, but it carries a whole throat full rather than one seed at a time. When it reaches what it feels is a secure spot, it disgorges the seeds to eat one at a time or to hide them, often under leaves on the lawn.

Some people don't like to see blue jays at their feeders because they feel the jays hog all the sunflower seeds. The blue jay's habit of taking seeds away and hiding them, however, guarantees that some animals that would never visit the feeder will benefit from it. (It also explains how sunflowers occasionally find their way into lawns.)

Some of the larger birds, like doves and pheasants, simply swallow sunflower seeds whole. The hard shells are softened in the crop, and then shells and kernels are ground in the gizzard.

At the bird feeder, you can not only learn what foods each species prefers, but you can deduce how each usually goes about finding food. The bird that usually feeds on the ground will scratch among the seeds with its feet as it searches for its favorites. Aerial feeders and birds that feed from vegetation will tend to move the seeds around with their beaks. When you have both kinds of birds, there won't be much seed waste. The seed that falls from the feeder to the ground will be pretty well eaten by the sparrows, doves and finches that prefer to feed there.

Observing the ground-feeding birds will show you how dominant instinct is in determining animal behavior. Even though a sparrow is standing ankle-deep in seed, it will still scratch with its feet. This behavior is a predetermined response to the sight of food. The bird cannot choose not to scratch for food even though scratching isn't necessary.

Another example of instinct at work can be seen in the responses of various birds and other animals to a predator at the feeder. When threatened by a Cooper's hawk, the cardinals will dive for thick cover, the doves will scatter and the chipmunk will freeze. The hawk can't follow the cardinals into the thick brush, it won't see the chipmunk as long as the animal doesn't move, and it can't pursue all the doves at once. None of these creatures thinks all that through, however — it simply does what it's programmed to do.

This example teaches us something about observation: what we see may be obvious, but we can be fooled by it. For another example, let's look at the visit of a brown creeper to the feeder. The brown creeper is an insect-eating bird that most people never see at a feeder. When one does come along, the obvious conclusion is that it's there to eat seeds. It's really there, however, to take advantage of a food source you didn't plan to provide: the spiders and insects that took up residence in the feeder while it was in summer storage. When the insects are gone, the bird will go, too.

Various birds will come and go at your feeder all winter. If you continue to feed and observe your visitors over several years, you'll learn which birds stay in Michigan all year and when to expect the migrating birds to pass through in spring and fall. You'll probably also get some insights into the role of predators in the ecosystem, and you'll have a front-row seat to the behavior changes that mark the beginning of the nesting season. This knowledge should add to your enjoyment of nature from your back door.

BACKYARD STREAMS:
AN OVERLOOKED RESOURCE

A STREAM OR CREEK THAT WANDERS THROUGH SUBURBAN backyards or farmers' fields has a lot to offer the backyard naturalist who's not afraid to get his/her feet wet.

But many of these streams go unexplored — and unfished, even though they often yield good-sized specimens of bass, pike, sunfish and other desirable species. Take a look at the stream in your neighborhood and you can easily see why such creeks are neglected.

To begin with, they wind through heavily developed or highly cultivated land. To get to them, you have to cross private property. At the bank, you may have to push your way through a tangle of willows and weeds and other vegetation. Any time after mid-May, your passage will stir up clouds of mosquitoes.

Once you reach the stream, the only way to explore it is to wade it. Wading streams is a traditional practice farther south, but not in Michigan. My habit of reserving a pair of old tennis shoes that I wear just for wading is foreign to my neighbors. But I find that having a pair of wading shoes makes it a lot easier to enjoy these streams.

A good mosquito defense is necessary, too. Mosquito repellents in lotion form are usually the best. Aerosol sprays are more pleasant but effective for a shorter time. Lightweight garments made of netting are also available and very comfortable. The netting is treated with a potent repellent and stored in an airtight bag until needed.

After you're in the stream — which, if it's not very wide, runs through a tunnel of intertwined greenery — you'll see why few people fish these streams. There's no room overhead to flail away with fishing lures or flies. To throw any kind of bait, you must be willing to lose a lot of hooks and spend some time getting untangled from the vegetation.

The rewards can be surprising.

I have caught or have been with people who have caught a 7¾-pound brown trout, a 6-pound pike and a 3-pound smallmouth bass, all from neighborhood creeks. A youngster I know took a very large tiger muskie from a designated drain near East Lansing.

What kinds of fish you find in these streams depends on what sort of lake or river they flow into or out of, the water quality and the water temperature. Water pollution control efforts in recent years have done a pretty good job of cleaning up streams that used to be little more than open sewers. Even steelhead and salmon can sometimes be found in creeks so shallow in most spots that their back fins break the surface as they wriggle along.

The trick in fishing these streams is to find the pockets where the habitat is good for fish. There the water will be somewhat deeper and plants or rocks or piles of junk will offer hiding places. The fish will lurk there, waiting for food to float downstream to them. Float your bait through these spots and you have a good chance of getting a strike, especially if the water is high but not muddy, as after a summer rain.

You don't have to fish these streams to enjoy them, of course. Wading and observing the wildlife that lives in or visits the stream can be lots of fun. It's cool under the canopy of vegetation, and you're likely to surprise some animals you ordinarily might not see, such as mink, raccoons, water birds and soft-shelled turtles. You may also see unusual fish or their nests, such as stonerollers, small fish that roll stones into a large pile for a nest. The flowers that bloom along the banks of streams will be different from the ones you generally see along roadsides or in the woods. And you may glimpse some birds that rarely visit your backyard.

These streams are often very fertile, supporting a wide variety of plant and animal life. Exploring them can be relaxing without being boring. If you're fishing, there's the challenge of finding a place to toss your bait without getting hung up in some overhanging willow.

Mostly, there's the chance to get acquainted with a side of nature and a part of your community that you may have been unaware of. I encourage you to share your new awareness with your neighbors — get them interested in the stream and what it has to offer. Then, if someone from outside should propose "stream improvements" — straightening the course of it, paving the banks with concrete, cleaning out the downed trees that provide the hiding spots for fish — yours won't be the only voice raised to defend and preserve it.

DYNAMIC HABITATS—CHANGING TO REMAIN THE SAME

OFTEN WHEN PEOPLE ENJOY SEEING SOMETHING IN NATURE, they want it to stay just the way it is so they can enjoy it again and again.

With living communities, however, often the only way to keep them the same is temporarily to change them.

Remember when the wildfires were raging in Yellowstone National Park and the debate was going on over whether to let the fires burn or try to control them? The argument for letting the fires burn was that it would clear out aging forestland and renew the forest and wildlife habitat. Without that renewal, the character of the forest and its wildlife would change. To keep it the same, then, would require a seemingly drastic short-term change.

Something similar happens in Michigan, though on a much smaller scale, every spring. Temporary wetlands, ponds and puddles in March, April and May host a fascinating array of wildlife ranging in size from nearly microscopic invertebrates to ducks.

One of the most obvious of the smaller creatures in spring ponds are fairy shrimp, also known as "sea monkeys". These shrimplike invertebrates become very abundant starting soon after the ice melts in March. By May, they may be as long as 2 inches. Then the ponds dry up in early summer and they're gone until the next spring.

A closer look may reveal tiny tadpole shrimp and clam shrimp. I'll never forget my first experience as a city boy finding what appeared to be miniature clams no bigger than my fingernail in the puddles in a rutted dirt road one spring. I was amazed to find these tiny clamlike organisms several miles from the nearest major body of water. (Later I found the same creatures high in the Blue Ridge Mountains.)

These same ponds and wetlands are very important to tree frogs, toads and salamanders because they mate and lay their eggs in the water and the eggs hatch and develop there.

The survival of these small animals depends not only on the pond's being there in the spring, but also on its drying up in the summer.

Some species that lay their eggs there are so well adapted to the wet and dry cycle of these temporary wetlands that their eggs may require the drying of the pond. Without it they don't survive.

All of the creatures that make use of temporary wetlands and ponds would be in trouble of another sort if those ponds became permanent. If water was present all year round, these areas would support aquatic predators such as water boatmen, damselflies and dragonflies, and fish. These could greatly reduce or even eliminate many of the other puddle dwellers.

If you want a demonstration of the abundance of life in these short-term wetlands, all you need to do is scoop up a jar full of water on a warm May day and examine it in good light. You'll probably see water fleas, aquatic mites and, with a little luck, some fairy or tadpole shrimp. Swish a large aquarium net through the water, and especially through any flooded grass, and you're sure to catch some of these creatures. Collect some of the bottom and you may scoop up some clam shrimp, too.

Bring some pond water indoors, put it in an aquarium, give it some light and let it warm up, and you'll see an impressive concentration of plant and animal life.

Of course, you don't have to do this to appreciate the population explosion going on in a nearby pond. Simply step outdoors on any mild April evening and you'll hear the frogs. The spring peepers are the earliest. They usually begin their spring song of "peep, peep, peep" in March or early April in southern Michigan. The chorus frogs chime in next. The most distinctive of these produces a rising trill that sounds like a fingernail running along the teeth of a plastic comb. Listen closely and you might hear the high pitched constant trill of the tree frog.

Much of the frog chorus on these spring nights comes from these vernal ponds. If these ponds existed all year round, predators would eliminate many of the frog and toad tadpoles.

The principle of changing to stay the same is true of many of the things we enjoy in nature — meadows, wetlands and forests. Periodic disturbance keeps them from evolving into something else. We don't have to have a forest fire to see this principle in action. We can see it in the vernal ponds that are part of nature from your back door.

NATURE FOR COMMUTERS

You CAN MAKE YOUR DRIVE BACK AND FORTH TO WORK MORE interesting, stay more alert and drive more safely by keeping your eyes open for wildlife as you travel.

You don't have to live in or drive through a rural area to see a great deal of wildlife as you commute. Especially in the fall, when birds are migrating and many mammals are moving about, you can see a variety of wild animals in the suburbs and even in the cities.

The largest animals you're likely to see are deer, and you're most likely to see them in early morning and in the evening around dusk. October, November, April and May are the months when deer are most likely to be seen along roadsides or crossing roads.

If you get into the habit of keeping your eyes moving from the road ahead to both sides of the road to your rear view mirror, you are likely to spot more deer and other wildlife than if you merely stare straight ahead. And you're less likely to be bored and half-hypnotized by the sameness of the road unrolling under your tires. By staying alert and observant, you're more likely to spot potential hazards — including deer poised to jump out in front of you from the side of the road — while you still have time to avoid them.

Be especially alert at deer crossing signs. These signs represent places where there have been a certain number of deer-automobile collisions, indicating that deer regularly cross the road there. But you can see deer anywhere, especially from September through December, when the breeding season and the activities of hunters have the animals stirred up and moving around, sometimes at odd times of the day, and in the early spring, when many feed on the newly sprouting vegetation.

Another group of animals you are more likely to see along the road than in your backyard are the predator birds. At any time of the year, you may see the red-tailed hawk and the kestrel or sparrow hawk. In the winter, the rough-legged hawk is also a possibility. Look for them at the tops of dead elm trees and utility poles. They perch there to scan the fields and roadsides for mice and other prey. Though you will rarely see one of these birds make a kill, you may see them soaring or diving toward the earth, or perhaps hovering over the freeway median by fluttering their wings into the wind.

You might think you'd see pheasants only in rural cornfields, but I frequently see pheasants in Detroit and Lansing along interstate highway rights-of-way. A few empty lots grown up to brush and weeds can also provide the pheasants with the cover and food they need to survive in the city.

If your drive to work takes you through a stretch of rural land, you may see numerous sandhill cranes. Unless you're alert, however, you may think they're parts of dead trees, old wooden fence posts, cornstalks, or even deer or horses. Michigan's largest birds are tall, they're the gray-brown of weathered wood, and unless they're moving, they can blend into the landscape, especially when the colors of fall predominate.

You may not have to drive very far outside of town to see these stately birds. I have seen them just outside of Lansing, Jackson and Ann Arbor.

One of the neat things to watch for in the fall is waterfowl. An occasional glance upward may reveal the V-shaped flight of a flock of Canada geese. Harder to see are the huge flocks of ducks that pass over Michigan. They fly very high.

I spotted a strange cloud on my way to MSU one fall day. I glanced at it, then glanced again a moment later and realized that it was either getting bigger and darker or it was losing altitude. In another moment I could tell that it was a flock of ducks — I estimated about 5,000 of them altogether. They descended into a cornfield along the side of the road to feed on the grain left behind by the harvesters.

There was a firm, wide shoulder along the road there and the traffic was light, so I pulled off and stopped to watch. Shortly four more cars stopped, and all of us stood alongside our vehicles watching the ducks about 100 yards away. The ducks in the back of the flock kept flying ahead of the leaders and settling down in the stubble to feed. As the back of the flock kept doing this, it looked as if the whole flock was rolling across the field. When it reached the end of the field, the flock took off, and we watchers got back in our cars and continued on our way.

A couple of my favorite wildlife observation posts are bridges I cross on my way to work. If traffic permits, I always glance down the streams both ways, and I'm often rewarded with a glimpse of herons and other wading birds and other waterfowl. Often when it's safe I stop and stand on the bridges and look down into the water. Depending on the stream and the time of year, I may see carp, bass, salmon or steelhead. Morning or evening is a good time to look, because you don't have the glare of the sun striking the water directly.

Night driving offers fewer opportunities to observe and identify wildlife because you're limited to what you can see in the beam of your headlights. The light reflected by animal eyes may tip you off to the presence of deer along the side of the road, or perhaps raccoons, opossums and other smaller animals. In an urban or suburban area, watch at the very fringe of the light from your headlights and you may get a good idea of the extent of the local rodent problem. Both mice and rats are likely to be moving around at night.

If you want to carry your observations of wildlife one step further, you can begin to note the patterns in the road kills. If you drive the same road day in and day out, you may see very few road kills for weeks and then all of a sudden a rash of them, generally all the same species. One week it may be opossums or skunks. In July, it's likely to be raccoons. In midsummer, the mother raccoon generally starts taking her young with her on her nightly excursions. Those that don't stick close to her often don't make it across the road.

Sometimes the patterns of animal movement are linked to the seasons; sometimes to the weather or some other factor. Mowing the roadsides in the early summer, for instance, generally results in a flush of new plant growth. Rabbits and groundhogs move in to take advantage of the tender forage and end up as road kill statistics.

Watching for such patterns in animal movement can lead to some insights about wildlife habits and behavior. It shouldn't lead you into unsafe driving practices, however. Watching for wildlife can help you stay alert and drive safely. But in the interest of safety, don't overdo it. If you spot something you want to observe more closely, pull off the road. If you can't do that safely, drive on. But don't gawk and stare and forget what you're doing. That's good advice that's easy to forget, especially if you're driving along Rt. 2 in the western U.P. and bald eagles are flying overhead or feeding on deer carcasses along the roadside.

To make your stops to observe wildlife more enjoyable, you may want to carry binoculars or a camera with a telephoto lens. Staying alert and being ready to watch or photograph the animals you spot as you drive to and from work can make your daily trek both safer and more interesting.

DEATH AS A PART OF LIFE

FALL IS A TIME OF YEAR WHEN THOSE OF US WHO ENJOY OBSERVING nature come face to face with something we may not like to think about: the fact that death is a big part of the natural scheme of things.

A great deal of animal mortality occurs in the fall. It may seem odd, at first, that so many animals die during September, October and November, when food and cover are abundant and the weather is generally mild. For animals in their second year, it generally is a lush time. But for animals in their first year of life, it's the time when they're just striking out on their own, independent of the parent or parents that raised them. It's also migration time and, for some animals, mating season, so a lot of animals are on the move, many for the first time, and through new territory. Both prey and predator populations are at their peak for the year, making it more likely that they'll run into one another. Animals are also likely to encounter members of their own species, so the spread of disease is another threat.

Homeowners are most likely to see animals killed by accidents and diseases.

Road kills are common sights in the fall, as young animals with no experience with automobiles fail to live long enough to acquire it.

You may see animals killed on the road that you otherwise rarely see at all. I have seen young foxes, for instance, cavorting and wrestling on a road, oblivious to my approaching car. Common animals such as opossums, raccoons and skunks are abundant in autumn and are frequently killed by cars.

Deer-car accidents peak in October and November as adult deer get caught up in the exuberance of the mating season and forget what they've learned about cars. Fawns following does that aren't paying attention to the traffic don't have experience of their own to warn them and so often collide with cars.

Among the scavengers that feed on road kills, it's the younger members that get killed. You rarely see an adult crow killed by a car, but you may see juvenile birds that didn't get out of the way fast enough to avoid an approaching car.

Young birds may also fly into the paths of cars. But many fatal accidents involving birds involve a stationary object.

Bird collisions with structures, especially windows, peak at this time of year. In rural areas, ruffed grouse may fly through picture windows as young birds looking for places to live see the reflection of the landscape in the window and mistake it for more of what they have been flying through. A 1-pound grouse flying at 30 miles per hour can do a lot of damage to a plate glass window. The bird is usually killed, too.

Migratory songbirds also fly into windows. Sometimes a whole flock will follow its leader into the glass. Night-flying migrating birds may be confused by the mercury vapor yard light near an isolated rural home and fly into the light, the post, surrounding trees or nearby structures. Homeowners may get up in the morning to find warblers, thrushes and members of other species dead or dying by the dozen in their yard.

Radio towers are also a hazard to migrating birds. People who live near such towers often find birds that have collided with them in the night, just as dwellers in high-rise apartment buildings may find the ground around their buildings littered with dead birds.

The homeowner usually doesn't see predators at work, though an occasional pile of feathers or a few tufts of fur may indicate where one has made a meal.

If you were to see some of the young predators in their first few weeks of independence, you probably wouldn't be impressed with their efficiency.

Though hiding and swooping on prey is pretty much instinctual behavior, the young raptors (hawks and other predatory birds) don't have any training or experience to go with it. Once they've caught something, they may not know what to do with it. And if the bird or animal screams or flutters or struggles a great deal, it may frighten the predator so much that it not only turns that individual loose but may never prey on that species again.

Young mammalian predators seem to have problems coordinating all the parts of the hunt: the stalk, the attack, the pounce and the kill. Probably only the fact that there are so many likewise inexperienced and inept prey animals around saves all these young predators from starving before they get their act together.

Though homeowners may not recognize it, they may see the effects of disease on local animal populations. Some years, distemper in the raccoon population means that a lot of people see raccoons acting strangely. Sometimes they die in urban and suburban backyards. Occasionally, trichomoniasis, a parasitic disease of doves, is seen. Affected doves may look normal, but the disease constricts their throats so that, unless some accident or predator gets them first, they eventually die of thirst or starvation. Doves that don't quite get out of the way of a car, or those that a predator surprises at the bird feeder, may have been weakened by the disease so they could not escape a quicker end.

Sometimes it's possible to reduce a specific kind of mortality. For instance, if you know from past years that your yard lights seem to attract large numbers of night-flying songbirds that then kill themselves flying into structures and trees, you might consider turning off or shading the brightest lights from mid-September until late October. Driving carefully from dusk 'til dawn may save not only a deer or two but a great deal of damage to your car.

Probably the only other time of year comparable to fall in animal mortality is the spring, when newborn animals are taking their first flights or first steps outside the den. In both the fall and the spring, the important thing for us to remember is that death is part of the natural scheme of things. We can't change that, so the thing to do is try not to worry too much about each individual animal but, where possible, to prevent avoidable and useless loss.

Chapter VI

Backyard Management Projects

NESTING BOXES FOR WILDLIFE

IF YOU WANT TO ATTRACT WILDLIFE TO YOUR HOME GROUNDS, SPRING offers a unique opportunity. Cavity-nesting birds of all sizes and colors are scouting around for suitable nesting places. By providing them, you may attract several kinds of birds to observe and enjoy.

A nesting box for birds can be as plain and simple or as elaborate as you like. A rough, wooden, unpainted, square box with a hole in it is just as likely to meet with some bird's approval as a miniature Victorian cottage with porches, windows and gabled roof. The birds that take up residence will depend on where you put the box and on the size of the opening in it.

For instance, a small — 5" x 5" x 8" — single house placed 4 to 6 feet above the ground on a fence post in the open away from trees makes a good home for bluebirds. The entry hole should be about 1½ inches across — large enough to let the bluebirds in easily but not large enough to let other, larger birds move in.

To attract purple martins, you need to supply an apartment house with many separate compartments. Plenty of ventilation is essential, and at least two sides of each compartment must be adjacent to outside air. This is necessary to keep the house from getting too warm inside. Painting the roof white to reflect the sun will also help keep it cooler. Place your martin house on a post

15 to 20 feet above the ground, out in the open and adjacent to water, if possible.

Purple martin and bluebird houses often become the homes of tree swallows initially. Like martins and bluebirds, tree swallows feed on flying insects. So, if one of your aims in attracting these birds is to take advantage of a little natural pest control, one species is as good as another.

All three of these birds are attractive to look at and interesting to watch. The male purple martin is an iridescent purple. The female is less purple, with a gray belly. In flight, purple martins have slightly forked tails and sharply backswept wings. The tree swallow has an iridescent green back and a white belly.

Smaller insect-eating birds that may be attracted by nesting boxes include chickadees, titmice, nuthatches and house wrens. Unlike the martins and swallows, which catch flying insects on the wing, these birds catch their dinner in your lawn, garden, trees and shrubs.

For chickadees and wrens, a single nesting box along the edge of a wooded or bushy area is ideal. To keep larger birds out, make the entry hole no larger than 1 inch for wrens and 1⅛ inches for chickadees.

Nuthatches and titmice prefer a box secluded in a clump of trees. A 1¼ -inch hole is best.

Though you could erect a post to fasten these houses on, any convenient tree trunk or large limb will do. Place them 5 to 20 feet off the ground.

An 8" x 8" x 15" box with a 3-inch opening, placed 10 to 20 feet above the ground in an open area, may attract a kestrel (sparrow hawk). These colorful birds — cream and white on the belly, with blue-gray wings and an orange-brown back, all marked with black spots and bars — do not feed heavily on sparrows, as the name implies. But they are fearsome predators of large insects and mice.

A nesting box in a barn is not likely to attract a barn owl in Michigan, but it may become home to a screech owl or saw-whet owl. These small owls, like kestrels, can be helpful in rodent

control. If you do not have a barn, a small clump or grove of trees will be suitable for a nest box.

The practice of using natural predators to reduce insect and rodent problems goes way back in history. The North American Indians used to use purple martins to repel crows from their corn patches. Martins defend their territory vigorously against crows and, to a lesser degree, against blackbirds. The Indians made purple martin houses by tying gourds to a cross-pole and fastening that to a tall, upright post to make the community nesting structure that martins like. The martins' preying on flying insects also helped reduce populations of mosquitoes and other pesky flying insects in the area.

They will do the same for you today, but it is unrealistic to think that putting up a martin house or attracting a kestrel to your yard is going to solve all your flying insect or rodent problems. These predators can help reduce the scope of the problem, however, so that other control methods can be more effective.

If you enjoy watching birds, you may feel that just having them around is enough return for your efforts. In either case, you will improve your chances of getting the birds you want if you put up several houses rather than just one. Nature will usually fill a birdhouse with something — but it may not be the animal you want! Squirrels, flying squirrels, other mammals, bees and hornets, and other species of birds may move into your nesting boxes. If you have erected several, you are more likely to see at least one occupied by the birds you want. And you can afford to be a little more tolerant of other tenants.

A STITCH IN TIME

March and April is the time of year when a whole lot of critters start moving into Michigan homes. Often the human occupants do not realize they have houseguests until much later, and by that time, the animals can be difficult to get rid of.

It is much easier to prevent an invasion by doing a little home maintenance during the pleasant weather in late summer and early fall.

If you live along a heavily wooded river, fall is the time to put a screen over the top of your fireplace chimney. In late March or early April, female raccoons go down chimneys looking for a place to have their young. The smoke shelf in your fireplace is an ideal spot. Chances are you will not know the raccoon family is in residence until May when the young start getting active and vocal.

A screen on your chimney will also keep out female wood ducks that will be looking for nesting cavities in May. Wood ducks are tree cavity-nesting ducks, and it is not uncommon for them to fall down chimneys in their quest for a nesting site.

Screening also keeps out chimney swifts. These interesting birds are usually no problem unless a windstorm tears their nest loose so that it falls down into the fireplace. Then you have several sooty, frightened birds loose in your house.

Starlings, squirrels and other animals that have learned to warm themselves in the exhaust air from your chimney may also fall into an unscreened opening. Getting them outdoors again can be a dirty adventure.

Fall is also a good time to make repairs to siding, eaves, roofs, window and door frames, and foundations. If you do not find and repair the holes and rotten spots, squirrels, bats and other little invaders are likely to find them for you.

If you have had trouble with rats, groundhogs, skunks or

possums digging under a shallow foundation, getting into a crawl space or under a porch, or making their home under a mobile home, early March is an excellent time to trap these animals and prevent this year's problems before they get started. Warming temperatures and melting snow mean these animals will be getting more active, but food supplies are still very short, so animals are easily enticed into box traps. If you wait until mid-April, there will be enough food springing up out of the ground that the animals will be able to turn up their noses at almost any goodies you might try to tempt them with. Another advantage of eliminating them now is that they will take their young with them. You will not have to worry about a nest of baby skunks or woodchucks either dying under the porch or surviving and staying around.

Often a skunk will have lived around your house all winter and escaped notice until it defended itself against harassment by another animal. The chances that a female raccoon or a family pet will have an encounter with mom skunk are greater now that all critters concerned are moving around more.

April is the month that many people think their homes are being invaded by snakes. What is actually happening is just the reverse — snakes that may have spent the winter in a cavity next to a rough basement wall emerge from hibernation and begin to spread out into the surrounding area. The homeowners may see last year's young snakes emerging and jump to the conclusion that a nest of snakes has hatched under the house. This is not the case, however, and it is one wildlife "problem" that solves itself very nicely.

Problems with the animals that actually do move into your

home do not go away so easily, however. You are ahead of the game to anticipate problems that are likely to develop and to handle them while they are still relatively easy to solve. Given the price of a home these days, and the cost of the energy needed to operate one, it may not be such a bad thing to be forced to keep the place repaired.

It is definitely easier to make the repairs and keep the animals out than to evict the critters and then try to keep them from coming back in. Squirrels that are driven out of a house, for instance, will try to gnaw their way back in where repairs were made to seal up their entry hole. Then you have no choice but to eliminate the squirrels. Better to replace the rotten board, prevent further deterioration to the house, save a little energy and keep the squirrels out in the first place.

Taking a "stitch in time" will also make it easier to continue to enjoy the animals that share your yard and neighborhood.

WOODPILES AND WILDLIFE

꙰

BURNING WOOD FOR HEAT IN FIREPLACES AND WOODSTOVES HAS become more commonplace in recent years. Some people are finding that the question of where to put the woodpile can lead to some unpleasant run-ins with wildlife.

Wherever you put it, a woodpile can provide cover for rats, mice, chipmunks, ground squirrels, and hordes of spiders, insects and other invertebrates. Under most circumstances, the mere presence of some of these creatures does not pose a problem and may even be enjoyable. In some locations, however, a woodpile is an invitation to trouble.

One of these is next to the dog pen. It is logical to want to concentrate the less attractive features of the backyard in an out-of-the-way spot where they will not dominate the landscape. If you look at it that way, putting the dog pen and the woodpile together toward the back of the lot makes a lot of sense. If you put the wood on the windward side of the dog pen, you can even provide a nice windbreak for the dog.

You are also practically guaranteeing yourself a rat problem.

Rats are constantly moving through your neighborhood in warm months, scrounging food and looking for likely places to settle down. Because most people tend to overfeed their pets, the uneaten or spilled food in and around the dog pen provides a readily available food source. A woodpile provides excellent cover. Place the woodpile next to the dog pen, and the rats will move right in.

If the food and cover are separated by 20 yards or so, you do not have a problem. The trip back and forth may take more energy than the rats could get from the food, or the danger of their being picked off by some owl, cat or other predator may be too great a risk. If you place the food and cover side by side, however, the rats can get food by expending very little energy and with very little risk. The result can be a severe rat problem.

The solution is easy: put the woodpile somewhere else.

Not next to the compost pile, however. Rats cannot live in a functioning compost pile because it is too hot. But if you stack your wood next to it, the rats will be delighted to live in the woodpile and scamper out to feed on the vegetable parings, leftovers and other food scraps you carry to the compost pile from your kitchen before the compost pile can decompose them.

Again the solution is to put the woodpile elsewhere.

Many people choose, for convenience, to place it on the back porch or next to the house where the roof overhang can protect it against rain and snow. Unless the foundation, siding, windows and doors, and exterior plumbing and utility fixtures of your house are as snug and tight as the door of a bank vault, however, it is only a matter of time until the creatures taking shelter in the wood move into the house with you.

It does not take a very big opening to admit a rat — only about ½ inch. A mouse can squeeze through a ¼-inch hole. Give these animals a good hiding place next to the house, and they will eventually find a way in.

The solution is to put the woodpile some distance from the house, so the animals that take shelter in it have a long, dangerous trek across the yard to get to the house, the dog food dish or the scraps in the compost pile. This will make life in your yard risky and inconvenient enough that they probably will not linger.

For your convenience, keep two or three days' worth of wood on the porch or in the carport. If you keep moving wood in and out, mice and other animals will not have a chance to settle in.

Store even this temporary supply of wood up off the ground, porch or pavement. Place a couple of cinder blocks and boards down and pile wood on top of them, or use one of those decorative wrought iron log hoops to hold the firewood. Get your main woodpile up off the ground, too. The wood itself will stay drier and be less likely to decay, and the woodpile will be less likely to become home to rodents and, in warm weather, snakes, if there is a gap between the bottom of the pile and the ground.

The potential problems with a backyard woodpile do not have to happen. All you have to do is think a bit about the creatures that inhabit and pass through your backyard and avoid making attractive places for them where they are likely to cause trouble. Then you can enjoy your wood fires and your view of nature from your back door.

CUTTING COSTS OF BIRD FEEDING

IN YEARS PAST, PEOPLE WHO WANTED TO FEED WILD BIRDS DURING the winter had little choice in the marketplace. Supermarkets would offer a wild bird seed mixture and maybe sunflower seeds in small bags, but to find the ingredients for custom seed mixtures or special items like thistle seed, people had to make the rounds of the local elevators and feed stores.

In recent years that has changed. Retailers of wild bird food are offering such a variety of feeds that the big challenge in feeding birds is no longer where to find the goodies but how to keep costs down.

Sunflower seed, rape seed, millet, cracked corn, thistle seed, peanut hearts, safflower seed, and a host of other seeds and grains are available in bulk in supermarkets, garden centers and other retail outlets. It is easy to get carried away with the variety and end up spending more than you can really afford.

There are a number of ways to control the costs of bird feeding, however.

One approach is to feed a mixture of 50 percent black oil-type sunflower seeds, 35 percent millet and 15 percent cracked corn. This mixture will attract the greatest variety of birds to your yard at the least cost.

If you want to draw other species to your feeding station, buy small quantities of some of the other feeds available and put them out separately, in special commercial feeders or in jar lids, used TV dinner trays, plastic bleach bottles and other recycled throwaways. See which birds come to each type of food and how much of each food is consumed. Then choose from these foods the ones you want to add to your basic mix or feed separately.

Some foods should not be mixed with others. Thistle seed, sunflower seed, safflower seed and peanut hearts are best fed separately. The reason is that the birds that prefer these foods will sort through a mixture to find them. In the process, they may waste large quantities of seed. It is usually OK to mix millet, cracked corn, wheat and sorghum because a variety of birds will eat all of them.

The design of your feeder can also help reduce feed waste. Best are the demand feeders, which release food only as it is consumed. They reduce the amount of feed that can be blown away, rained or snowed on, or soiled. Birds can learn to rake out the rest of a mixture to get at the occasional sunflower seed or other favorite food, however, so a separate sunflower seed feeder is advised.

If you fill your feeders whenever the contents get low, you will find yourself feeding more and more birds at an ever increasing cost. To keep costs down and eliminate the possibility that you will have to give up feeding altogether, put your birds on a diet by setting up a budget for bird food.

Decide how much you want to spend, either for the entire winter or on a monthly or weekly basis. Then figure out how much seed that amount of money will buy and divide the quantity of seed by the number of days or weeks that the food must last. Then portion it out accordingly. And be firm! A bird food budget is worthless if you do not stick to it.

Though it may be difficult at first to see the feeders standing empty half the day, it is better for the birds to put out some food every day from December through April or early May than to start to feed in December but run out of money and stop after a blizzard in February. Under severe weather conditions, birds may not have an alternate source of food, unless your neighbor also feeds birds. For sure, you will miss some unusual bird activity.

Even the best laid plans for a bird feeding budget may be foiled by squirrels. Especially when the ground is frozen and they can not retrieve the nuts they have stashed, squirrels may take over a bird feeding station.

Making a feeder squirrel-proof is a difficult task. If you put the feeder where you can get to it to fill it, the squirrels can get to it to empty it. Metal squirrel guards to keep squirrels from climbing a post or tree to the feeder have to be at least 4 feet off the ground and at least 18 inches wide. If the squirrels can jump to the feeders from nearby trees, utility wires or buildings, you will need metal or

plastic umbrella-shaped guards above the feeders, too.

One fairly reliable way to thwart the squirrels is to put a wire cage over the feeder. Use wire mesh with holes that little birds can walk through and bigger birds can reach through to get food. The squirrel can eat the food that is already out, but he cannot bring any more down.

Squirrel-proofing your bird feeder may be more successful if you provide squirrels with their own food supply elsewhere in your yard. Ear corn stuck on nails on a platform or post, or a few black walnuts or hickory nuts placed where the squirrels can find them each day will help divert them from the bird feeders.

To increase the number and variety of birds visiting your feeding station without greatly increasing the expense of feeding, supply birds with a source of unfrozen water. Even when snow is on the ground, you will find birds flocking to your yard for a drink. A supply of grit — canary or parakeet gravel — may be even more popular. When the soil is snow covered or frozen, your feeder may be the only source of the grit that birds need to digest their food.

Lastly, where you buy your bird food may be a big factor in its cost. Elevators and feed mills generally offer the lowest prices on bulk seed, but sale prices at garden centers and other retail outlets are often competitive. Local bird clubs and nature centers may buy bird food in large quantities and pass the savings along.

Keeping costs in line will make it easier and more enjoyable to feed and observe the birds in the winter.

Chapter VII

Human Nature

VIEWPOINT COLORS
EXPERIENCES WITH WILDLIFE

SOMETIMES THE MOST INTERESTING AND OCCASIONALLY frustrating aspect of my work with wildlife is observing the ways humans react to situations involving animals.

Take the person who called my office wanting to know what to do about a fox on her property. I asked about pets or livestock, and she told me she had neither for the fox to get mixed up with. She asked about foxes attacking people, especially children, and I assured her that foxes don't bother people, even little people, and that rabies in Michigan foxes is really a rarity. As the conversation went on, she realized that she didn't really have a problem with the fox and that the chance to catch a glimpse of it on her property was actually kind of exciting.

Another woman called me not long ago about a rabbit that was digging holes in her yard. Rabbits don't ordinarily dig holes, so I went to investigate. I found that the rabbit had hollowed out a shallow depression and was nesting in it. Without realizing what she had been watching, the homeowner had observed the rabbit lining the depression with fur, nursing her young and cleaning the nest.

Once she understood what she'd been seeing and saw the

baby rabbits close up, the costs of having the rabbit there — a small blemish in the lawn and about $3 worth of repellent to keep the mother rabbit from nibbling on her flowers — shrank away to almost nothing in the face of the opportunity to watch the rabbit rear her family. By the time this realization had sunk in, however, I had already emptied the nest of babies and fur lining and suggested filling in the depression with soil and sprinkling a little grass seed and water on it to restore the perfection of the lawn. When I couldn't restore the nest and young, the woman saw that the perfect lawn was merely empty.

I saw the same sort of thing happen when I pulled some baby raccoons off the smoke shelf in a fireplace. When the family that lived in the house saw the kitten-sized raccoons and understood what all the noise in their chimney had been about, they decided that it was almost OK to have raccoons in the chimney. If the animals had been just a little less noisy, they wouldn't have minded at all, especially after they learned that the raccoon family would have left as soon as the little ones were agile and strong enough to follow mother raccoon up and out of the chimney. They could see the situation as a temporary visit by the raccoons rather than an invasion.

I've seen this sort of thing happen time and again: knowing what's happening — instead of only imagining what might be going on — often changes the way people view the situation. Even if they don't come to appreciate it as a positive experience, they can at least make decisions about what to do about it more calmly and rationally.

This isn't always true, of course. When bats and snakes are involved, for instance, many people are caught up in an irrational

■

fear that no amount of knowledge can counter. The fact that a black snake eats a lot of mice doesn't matter — it's still a snake, and the terrified homeowner would rather have the mice in the house than the snake in the yard.

Actually, the mice are a bigger threat than the snake could ever be. Mice are very destructive in the home. Their constant gnawing can damage the house and materials in it, including electrical wiring, which may then start a fire. Mice also carry the organisms responsible for several serious diseases. So mice in the house are definitely a cause for alarm and action.

Mice don't instill the fear in many people that bats and snakes do, however, even though the costs of coexisting with mice can be very high. When the image of the cute little pink-eared mouse is put alongside the Dracula connotations associated with bats, to most people, the mice are going to look more appealing.

Maybe that's just human nature. If so, it's a major factor in the way we see nature from the back door.

THE EYE OF THE BEHOLDER

WHEN FREQUENT RAINS IN JUNE PREVENT REGULAR MOWING, the display of hawkweed can be exceptionally beautiful. Some fields I pass going back and forth to work rival wildflower scenes out of National Geographic.

Finding one particularly attractive display being mowed one day — before I had a chance to photograph it — got me thinking about how a positive or negative attitude toward some aspect of our environment can drastically affect how we respond to it.

Take the hawkweed, for instance. The operative word is "weed." Those fields of gorgeous yellow and orange blossoms are often mowed rather than maintained and enjoyed because the property owners consider the plants weeds rather than wildflowers. States such as Michigan, Texas and Ohio have gone to some expense and effort to plant roadsides to wildflower mixtures. But let these same plants spring up in someone's lawn and they're considered pests that must be eradicated.

You could say that one person's weed is another's wildflower. Or maybe the same person would appreciate the plant if it were growing in another place.

Take dandelions. If they just grew along roadsides or in

meadows instead of lawns, people would probably value them as wildflowers — or at least not condemn them as noxious weeds. Likewise, the marsh marigold, which blooms so prolifically in spring along streambanks and roadside ditches, would be seen in a totally different light if it invaded suburban lawns.

In my lawn, one corner has gone gradually over to hawkweed, with my encouragement — I don't mow that area from the time the flower buds appear until the plants have gone to seed. I enjoy looking at the orange and yellow blossoms, and it's one area I don't have to mow — for part of the summer, anyway.

When I look at that area, I see wildflowers that I wish would spread faster and finish filling in that corner of the yard. When I showed a slide of the hawkweed to a College Week class at Michigan State University, one of the participants characterized it as a spreading weed.

In this case, what you see depends on what you want. I want less grass to mow and interesting flowers to look at. Someone else, who wants only grass, would see my wildflowers as undesirable. I'm prejudiced in favor of the hawkweed in my yard, while someone else may be prejudiced against anything that isn't grass.

The best example of this kind of prejudice in operation is the vastly different ways many people respond to two somewhat similar creatures: the robin and the ring-necked snake.

The robin, the state bird of Michigan, has a brownish back and a rusty orange breast and eats worms. The first robin seen in the spring is often greeted with joy as a harbinger of winter's end.

As anyone who has ever raised strawberries or cherries can

tell you, however, the robin also eats fruit. In late June and July, when the first batch of young robins is just getting out into the world, the destruction of fruit in a backyard garden or even a commercial planting can be significant.

A pair of robins in the backyard in spring is often welcomed, but few people are glad to see a huge flock of migrating robins settle into their neighborhood. Southern holly growers are particularly unhappy about the visitors from the north because they eat the red holly berries and then whitewash the green leaves.

In addition to being noisy, destructive and messy, robins will also bite if handled. They can't do much damage, but if they get a grip on your skin, they can give it a painful pinch, especially if they grab hold and then twist.

Now let's compare the robin to the ring-necked snake.

Like the robin, it is brown on the back with a reddish belly. The color pattern is almost identical. The main difference is that

the snake has an attractive white or yellow ring around its neck, like that of a pheasant or mallard.

Like the robin, the ring-necked snake eats worms. Unlike the robin, the ring-necked snake is one of the gentlest of animals. It avoids human contact if it possibly can, but if it's picked up, it makes no attempt to threaten, bluff or bite. With handling, it seems to come to enjoy the warmth of the human hand.

How ironic that, because of people's prejudice against snakes, this gentle, beneficial, harmless animal is regarded with fear and loathing, while the robin — noisy, messy, destructive and pugnacious — is so highly regarded that it's been selected as Michigan's state bird.

Obviously, the preceding descriptions are extremely biased. Neither creature fully deserves the way I have described it. But I wanted to demonstrate how prejudice can be used to create an unfair or even false characterization of wildlife.

We need to put our prejudices aside when we look at the environment in which we live. The alternative is to let our prejudices color what we see and how we relate to it. The problem with that is that, in the environment as in human society, maintaining and acting on our prejudices can be destructive. Just think of all the innocent, harmless snakes that get chopped to bits with shovels every year, just because people have never learned to see beyond their irrational dislike for snakes. This is a good example of how prejudice destroys. It's just one of the lessons we can learn from observing nature from your back door.

DEALING WITH FEAR

In teaching about natural resources and wildlife, I meet people — adults and young people — who fear things associated with natural resources and the out-of-doors. Each summer, I participate in the Great Lakes Natural Resources Camp, where, in addition to teaching about natural resources, we involve the 4-H'ers in natural resource-based recreation and teaching. In doing so, we encounter lots of fears: fear of the water, fear of heights, fear of snakes, fear of the dark, fear of speaking in front of people.

In helping people deal with their fears, I have noticed that some people are consciously afraid — they fear one of these things and they know it. Some others are not afraid on a conscious level, but when they get into a situation that evokes one of these fears, they experience shortness of breath, rapid heartbeat, narrowing of vision — all the classic fear symptoms — and sometimes even lose consciousness.

Some of these people get angry or impatient with themselves when this happens. Consciously they know there is no reason for this reaction to occur, but they can't control it, and they take themselves to task over it. Or they ask why, if they are not afraid of the situation, do they experience these disturbing reactions to it? And what can they do to overcome their fear?

Through years of experience and reading, I've come to believe that there are two ways to tackle these fears. For fears on the conscious level — those things you fear and know you fear — the first step is information and education. Become familiar with whatever is causing this reaction and observe others dealing successfully with it or even enjoying it. When you see others revelling in high places, the water, the dark or snakes, you can begin to dismantle your conscious fear. You may even eventually come to enjoy a situation that you would once have found terrifying.

The second step is to give yourself a chance to overcome your unconscious fear gradually, through safe, protected exposure to whatever you're afraid of.

One of the experiences that I deal with at camp is kids getting to know wildlife, particularly snakes. A lot of people are afraid of snakes all out of proportion to any threat they pose. In Michigan, we have 17 native snakes, and only one, the massasauga rattlesnake, is venomous. None will bite unless attacked; some make no attempt to bite unless injured. Yet more often than not, many people who encounter snakes will go out of their way to kill them, simply because they are snakes. Others are so frightened at the mere sight of a snake that they literally pass out if a snake slithers across their path.

At natural resources camp, we had all kinds of campers, from those who liked snakes and didn't hesitate to handle them to others who didn't want to be in the same room with a snake in an aquarium. By the end of the week, some kids who had started the week absolutely terrified of snakes were no longer consciously afraid of them and had largely overcome their unconscious fear reaction. One little girl had overcome her irrational fear to the extent that she could actually enjoy holding a snake, though she still couldn't bring herself to reach into the aquarium of snakes to get one out.

What happened? The campers received information on the nature and behavior of snakes, and the ones who were reluctant to touch the creatures at first observed the others handling and enjoying them. Repeated touching of the snakes lessened their fear reaction to the point where they could master it.

You don't have to go to a special camp to overcome fears. You may not even have to leave your backyard.

You may not live near water or a high place or have too many public speaking opportunities there, but your backyard does get dark at night. And no matter where you live in Michigan, if you have a vacant lot nearby, even in downtown Detroit, there is a chance you will encounter a snake someday.

---

* Michigan State University has published "Michigan Snakes", a full-color book on the 17 snakes native to Michigan. In addition to color photos of each species, it provides information on where they occur, what they eat, how they reproduce, and whether they're shy and gentle or nervous in temperament. The book is on sale at your local county Cooperative Extension Service office.

If you would like to learn about snakes to help you overcome your fear or nervous reaction to them, getting a good field guide will help*. As you read this publication and perhaps use it to identify a snake you've just seen, it will help you overcome your conscious fear. Overcoming an unconscious fear reaction will probably require the help of a friend who can set up a non-threatening situation in which you can gradually get acquainted with a harmless snake.

If you or a member of your family is afraid of the dark, August would be a good time to begin to conquer that fear. A fantastic display of meteors that should peak around Aug. 12 makes this a good time to get a few friends or family members together, sit outside in lawn chairs at night and watch the heavenly show. If you can get away from city lights, the viewing can be spectacular. (We watched at camp, and we found it's hard to be afraid of the dark with friends all around watching meteors flash across the starry sky.)

Even as you're overcoming fear of snakes or fear of the dark, or helping someone else do so, you need to recognize that there are venomous snakes and dangerous situations, persons and things in the dark that need to be avoided. The ability to distinguish between these real dangers and irrational fears is just one more thing you can learn as you observe nature from your back door.

---

* If you want to learn more about the night sky, contact Abrams Planetarium at MSU in East Lansing at (517) 355-4676.

HUMAN ATTITUDES

ONE OF THE INTERESTING ASPECTS OF NATURE IN YOUR YARD IS human nature as it relates to wildlife and the natural environment. Human attitudes and behavior toward wildlife vary greatly with the individual, ranging from irrational fear to implacable hate to uncompromising love.

To some people, any experience with wildlife is negative. These are the people who would want to get rid of a purple martin house because they don't like to hear the martins singing, or a family of chipmunks because they don't like to see them running around the yard.

On the other extreme is the person who wouldn't take action against a woodchuck that was undermining her porch supports so that the whole porch was falling off the house. Though she wanted to get rid of it — by driving it away with noise or chemicals — she would not permit it to be trapped and released elsewhere because she didn't want to subject the animal to that kind of stress.

This attitude reflects some romantic notions people have about individual animals. We have humanized them so much that we often lose track of the fact that an animal — whether it's a baby rabbit or a woodchuck or a frog — is a biological machine for processing the food it eats into food for something else: a hawk, a snake, the neighborhood cat or another baby. Nature produces enough baby rabbits or whatever that a few of them live long enough to produce more, while the rest provide food for other organisms.

Between these two extremes in attitude are the people who feel fairly neutral toward wildlife. They don't have anything against wild animals, but they don't want to become involved with them, either. So, when they find a killdeer's nest in the lawn, they call someone else to solve the problem. That usually amounts to a death sentence for the young birds. They are difficult to raise in captivity, and if the nest is moved, the parents can't recognize it as theirs. But, because the person hasn't become personally involved in either preserving or destroying the birds, he's maintained his neutrality.

Sometimes people have a positive attitude toward wildlife but a negative experience that changes it. Take the robin, our state bird. Everybody likes robins — after all, they look pretty, they sing and they eat bugs. They also eat strawberries — and cherries and blueberries — and that makes them none too popular with home gardeners who grow these crops. Watching two robins raising a nest of young on a windowsill can be very exciting for the whole family. But finding a nest in the grill of your antique car, in the nail can in the tool shed (when you'd finally gotten around to nailing down that loose step!) or in some other place where the droppings, grass and mud of the nest can make things unpleasant, puts a different light on the subject.

Likewise, chipmunks are cute — until you find them in your pantry. Wood ducks are beautiful — until one falls down your chimney and wipes its sooty wings all over your freshly painted dining room. A family of raccoons is lots of fun to watch — until it takes up residence in your attic or chimney.

Some people are simply afraid of wild animals. Sometimes the fear grows out of a lack of understanding of animal behavior. Other times, it is irrational and unbounded.

The story of a friend's sparrow hawk (kestrel) illustrates the first kind of fear. He raised the orphaned falcon from a baby and taught it to hunt so that it could fend for itself. Then he turned it loose. Within a few days, I received a call from someone who wanted to know if birds ever got rabies. As soon as he told me what the bird looked like and what it was doing, I knew it was this fellow's kestrel.

The caller said the bird kept diving at him and clawing at his head and arm. Naturally he put up his arm to shield his head — which is just what you do when you want a trained falcon to land on your arm. When the bird put his feet out to land, the person interpreted it as an attack.

Irrational fears of animals afflict many people. I used to think that snakes, bats and spiders were the most feared, but I've found that many people are terrified of various kinds of animals. For example, some people are afraid of birds but love furry mammals, while others are afraid of mammals but like birds. Others may fear anything that wiggles — like worms and caterpillars — or anything that flies. An extreme example of this kind of fear is the person who is so afraid of snakes that she won't even walk into a laboratory where snakes preserved in alcohol are stored. Another is the man who set his house on fire trying to kill a harmless milk snake by pouring gasoline on it.

People whose attitudes toward wildlife don't fall into any of these extreme categories will probably have both good and bad experiences with wild animals. This illustrates something I think is very important. Living with wildlife is like living with people — occasionally you're going to encounter a troublesome individual. Usually, however, trouble with wild animals is not the animals' fault — at least, not completely. Animals that blunder down the chimney would not get in if there were no openings for them to enter by. Robert Frost said, "Good fences make good neighbors." Barriers that exclude wildlife make them good neighbors, also.

This brings us to another principle: what's good for people is usually good for wildlife. Take the business of raccoons getting into the house. The openings they use to come in are also letting a lot of heat out in the winter. If you close these openings to prevent the animals from getting in where they can do damage that may result in their being killed, you also save energy and money. And it may limit your experiences with wildlife to more pleasant ones.